FEARLESS PARENTING MAKES CONFIDENT KIDS

SHULAMIT BLANK

ORLY FUCHS-SHABTAI

FEARLESS PARENTING MAKES CONFIDENT KIDS

SHULAMIT BLANK

ORLY FUCHS-SHABTAI

SAMUEL WACHTMAN'S SONS

DEKEL ACADEMIC PRESS

Fearless Parenting Makes Confident Kids

Shulamit Blank & Orly Fuchs-Shabtai

Dekel Academic Press
www.dekelpublishing.com

North American rights by
Samuel Wachtman's Sons, Inc.
ISBN 978-1-888820-60-7

English Translation: Shulamit Blank
Language Editing: Katie Roman
Proof Reading: Ruti Frankel

Cover image: ©iStock.com/pixdeluxe

Cover design and typesetting by

For information contact:

Dekel Publishing House
P.O. Box 45094
Tel Aviv 6145002, Israel
Tel: +972 3506-3235
Fax: +972 3506-7332
Email: info@dekelpublishing.com

Samuel Wachtman's Sons, Inc.
2460 Garden Road, Suite C
Monterey, CA 93940, U.S.A.
Tel: 831 649-0669
Fax: 831 649-8007
Email: samuelwachtman@gmail.com

To our children.

Table of Contents

Introduction

Most parents love their children and want only what is best for them. We wrote this book for them.

This book was written for mothers and fathers who feed, diaper, and dress their children and who hold them in their arms through long nights of painful teething. It is dedicated to parents who are thrilled by the sight of their child's first steps and those tiny hands held out toward them, but who become confused and troubled when it comes to setting boundaries.

What do we mean by setting boundaries? Why are "boundaries" so important? What harm can be caused when there are no boundaries? Are punishment and boundaries one and the same? Is it a good idea to threaten a child with punishment? Would the setting of boundaries cause a child to feel defeated, misunderstood, or insulted? Can boundaries break a child's spirit? Can they hurt the child? Is there any sort of overall magic formula for raising children?

Our book deals with all these issues.

This book was written out of the awareness that setting boundaries for a child does not constitute a purely technical reaction, but is the result of a unique understanding of a child's needs. It is not easy for parents to set boundaries for their child, which is why it is important that they understand what their child goes through once they have embarked on the process. It is important for parents to remain aware of the significance of boundaries to a child and also of the intense potential damage that can be caused to a child who does not have boundaries set for him or her.

"The emperor has no clothes!" shouts the child. And indeed it seems inconceivable that while attitudes toward children have become more lenient and gentle, children have somehow turned more violent. Actually, one would have expected the complete opposite. Could we have all been wrong?

This book deals openly and boldly with matters of power and control and presents the issue of setting boundaries in a way that does not moralize; rather it delves into issues of tempestuous feelings and struggle, as well as personal development and self-awareness.

Chapter One

When There Are No Boundaries

On April 20, 1999, two teenage students, Eric Harris and Dylan Klebold, killed a teacher and twelve fellow students in a planned shooting rampage at Columbine High School in Colorado. The two boys then committed suicide. This was considered the worst-ever incident of school violence in the US. Had there been signs leading up to this tragedy?

Two years earlier, in 1997, the dean of students suspended both boys for hacking into the school's computer system and stealing locker combinations. In the police report, the dean pointed out that the boys' parents protested the suspensions. While Harris's parents were critical of the punishment because of their son's "minor" involvement, Klebold's father expressed his disagreement with suspensions in general. Also in 1997, police found a website on which the boys boasted about building pipe bombs. The police were sufficiently concerned to write out an affidavit for a search warrant, but they never filed it.

In 1998, Harris and Klebold were arrested for breaking into a van and stealing electrical equipment. In court, the boys made such a good impression that the juvenile judge offered to expunge their criminal records if they agreed to attend a diversionary program and stay out of trouble.

As time went by, the boys' rage continued to fester. They continued to misbehave, but received only minor reprimands. Dylan Klebold was sent to the dean's office again in1998 after he tried to deface a locker door. Working together, the boys produced a graphically violent video for a school project. They were not punished despite their teachers' complaints.

Both sets of parents expressed unmitigated shock when they found out that their sons were murderers. Tom Klebold said he rarely visited his son's room and was unaware that a few nights before the attack Harris had come to spend the night at the Klebold home. It was then that the two boys put together a video in which they boasted of their weapons cache and their murderous plan.

In interviews that appeared in the media following the event, the public was given the impression that both youths grew up in stable families and enjoyed love and warmth from their parents. Neighbors and acquaintances of the families described both sets of parents as supportive of their sons. "Dylan did not do this because of the way he was raised," his mother Susan said in an interview to the *New York Times*. "He did it in contradiction to the way he was raised." Were these parents in denial? Why was no one able to foresee that these boys were headed for trouble? Why had so many signs been ignored?

Tom Klebold asserted to police investigators that he and his wife were not absentee parents and that they loved their son and were always there for him. Is that true, and if true, is it enough?

The conventional educational and psychological approach in our society emphasizes the importance of warmth and love, tenderness, forgiveness and acceptance, and is reluctant to impose limits.

But are love and support enough? If this is how it turns out, where have we all gone wrong?

Perhaps the accepted approach is wrong?

Perhaps violent behavior, violation of the law, and defiance of morality are a direct result of the submissiveness of parents and teachers, and their fearfulness?

The Columbine mass shooting and expressed violence in families, in schools, and on the streets in many western countries compel us all to deal with these challenging questions.

Power! Control! Throughout childhood, children test the boundaries of authority and engage in struggles against parents, teachers, and authoritative establishments. Can it be that violence and crime are a direct result of parents' and teachers' weakness and, as a result, alienation and neglect that lead to their surrender to the unacceptable behavior of the children they have been charged to raise and educate? Is it possible that parents in our postmodern world are in denial about who their children are, or afraid to ask questions?

Let's look at the recent massacre in Newtown. A lot of what we have learned from Columbine could possibly have helped us prevent what happened in Newtown. We have to acknowledge that the human brain is capable of producing horror, and that knowing everything about the perpetrator, his family, the limits he was subjected to, his social experience, and the world he inhabits does answer the question "Why?" in many ways that could generate good policy and eventually resolve the problem.

Why didn't the Klebolds search Dylan's room and find his writings, and why didn't they track him to where he'd hidden his guns? Why wasn't Nancy Lanza, the mother of the Newtown shooter, more intrusive with her son? In our view, lack of intrusiveness and boundary setting is synonymous with neglect.

In today's western society, the general approach to raising children places emphasis on warmth and love, gentleness, forgiveness, and acceptance rather than on boundary setting and tough demands. Clearly, the three boys mentioned above had parents who raised their sons with warmth and love and were also especially permissive and forgiving. Is it conceivable that warmth and love are not enough and that being permissive and forgiving might breed violence?

Could the accepted approach be wrong?

The Colorado massacre, the Newtown massacre, and many other expressions of aggression and violence at home, in schools, and on the streets of western countries demand that the educational and psychological establishments join forces to find a solution for these critical issues.

The late Dr. Milton Erikson (1901–1980), an American psychiatrist well known for his unconventional approach to psychotherapy, had no compunctions about addressing this issue and developed a method that differed from the accepted and familiar one.

According to Erikson, setting boundaries is of supreme importance to the development of a child. With no boundaries imposed on him, the child feels himself to be stronger than his parents and, despite the heady thrill he gets from this feeling, he still has to pay a very heavy price because deep down he somehow feels that he is unable to cope with reality on his own. Erikson was convinced that a parent's weakness undermines a child's sense of security and exposes him to the dangers of intense anxiety. Erikson did not hesitate to advise parents to adopt firm measures in order to reinstate their authority.

The following case (1-1)[1] represents a sample of Erikson's approach.

A young divorced woman with three children turned to him for help in dealing with her eight-year-old son. She told Erikson that shortly after her divorce, her son underwent a drastic change in behavior. He started to misbehave in school, vandalized property both in school and at home, insulted his fellow students, refused to do his homework, was rude to his mother, quarreled with his sisters, broke neighborhood shop windows, disturbed the neighbors, and destroyed gardens. His mother's attempts at punishing him had no effect on him and he announced that nothing could stop him. At that point, the desperate woman turned to Erikson and acted on his advice.

On Saturday morning she sent her daughters to their grandparents' and stayed at home alone with her son. She placed a thermos of coffee on a table in the living room alongside a container of fruit juice, a telephone, a book, and a towel. The boy walked into the living room and demanded his breakfast. He was asked to wait for a while and reacted by raising a precious object and threatening to smash it on the floor if he didn't get his breakfast immediately. His mother caught his arm and forced him to lie down on his stomach and sat on him. For two hours he tried to free himself from

1 This number and the rest that follow refer to this book's endnotes.

her grasp, alternatively cursing her and begging her to let him go. After two hours, he stopped trying to pull himself free and appealed to her in a quiet voice to please get up and release him. She refused. She told him it wasn't time yet, picked up a book and started reading and even spoke to her friends on the phone. Another hour went by and the boy asked to go to the bathroom; his mother refused. The boy cried and begged. His mother didn't give in and told him to wipe himself with the towel. He made a further unsuccessful attempt to pry himself free of her and this time he wet his pants. An hour later, his mother agreed to free him.

The following day, for the first time in many months, the boy sat down to do his homework, tidied his room, and spoke politely to his mother and sisters. That very same day he went—on his own initiative—to the neighbors and local shopkeepers he had previously upset and asked for their forgiveness. His behavior became acceptable and has remained so ever since. Years later, no further emotional or behavioral problems were observed in him.

Not long after this event, when the mother was about to remarry, the boy asked for a meeting with Dr. Erikson to consult him about the man his mother chose to be her husband and his stepfather. Although he knew that his mother had acted according to Dr. Erikson's instructions, the harsh experience had not caused him to see the doctor as abusive or humiliating; on the contrary, he saw him as a man he could consult, a man who inspired confidence, a man who could be trusted and be relied upon.

Is it possible that the force the mother imposed on her son caused such far-reaching a change in his behavior in only one day?

How can we explain the boy's lightning-swift change, from completely unruly behavior to someone who is decent and moral (1-2), and why would the boy wish to hear the opinion of a man who set his mother "against" him?

Is there a connection between boundary setting and the development of moral inhibitions?

How can boundaries help a child channel his energies toward behavior that is positive and helpful?

These questions will be dealt with at length in this book.

First, we shall study the meaning of boundaries and how to set them, and try to understand why so many parents find it so hard to impose boundaries on their children. We shall also analyze the "contribution" of modern society to this hardship.

Chapter Two

"Am I a Good Parent?"

Few people are unfamiliar with the term "boundaries." Much is said about the importance of boundaries, but very little thought is given to **why** they are so important and **why** parents find it so hard to impose them.

What is a boundary?

In our everyday life, we tend to think of boundaries as signals to "stop" or "halt here!" In other words, we mean to say: "No! You mustnot! You cannot!"

If we want to cross a boundary between two countries, we need a special permit, and if we don't get it, we might be punished severely. Shouldn't it be the same in a family setting?

And what should be said about **setting** boundaries? Does this constitute the parents' announcement that a boundary exists, or does it indicate a "de facto" act on the part of parents that their child must behave within predetermined boundaries?

It is not a matter of semantics. There is a significant difference between knowing what boundaries are and actually acting within them (2-1). All too often we encounter children—and adults—who know what accepted boundaries are, but have no compunctions about crossing those boundaries.

All too frequently we witness troubling displays of children behaving wildly, fighting and harassing each other, while their parents stand by helplessly, saying things like, "Danny, honey, you shouldn't hit other kids, it's not nice, it hurts. Stop it, sweetheart." And nothing happens. Danny simply goes on doing what he apparently shouldn't be doing.

Let us, therefore, separate this into two distinct acts: *setting boundaries* and *imposing boundaries*.

When a parent announces the existence of a boundary and the child acts accordingly, this constitutes *setting boundaries*. When, on the other hand, the child fulfills the requirement of a boundary only after a power struggle that involves punishment, this is a case of *imposing boundaries* (2-2).

The term *setting boundaries* can be confusing, as many parents believe that it is sufficient to announce the existence of a boundary in order for it to be obeyed. Reality teaches us that these declarations and demands often have no effect whatsoever on the behavior of a child. When parents declare that boundaries are about to be set, many children interpret these words as no more than advice; only after boundaries are actually enforced, which usually happens only after a lengthy and repeated struggle, do these children respect these boundaries.

Since children are different from each other in temperament, it is possible that within one family some children obey the boundaries set for them and others change their behavior only after boundaries have been imposed. From this point forward, the term *setting boundaries* includes both the act of creating and announcing a boundary as well as imposing it.

The very act of setting boundaries can arouse fears and misgivings. As parents, it is clear to us that our children will not react with shouts of joy to the setting of boundaries. Sometimes, especially when we deal with difficult children, it might be met with opposition, anger, insult, and even tears, and, since our children are very dear to us, we cannot help but identify with their pain and frustration.

After all, we ourselves were once children and we also found ourselves facing angry and forbidding parents. Back then we thought if only…if only our parents were sufficiently understanding, patient, permitting, everything would be different—it would be much better. And now, we find ourselves in our parents' shoes having to cope with the difficult, frustrating, and disappointing job of being parents.

Setting boundaries for our children is very hard on us. That's not what we dreamed about when we visualized our relationships with our kids. We imagined caring for our children, playing with them, comforting them, or being amazed by them. We imagined an experience of friendship, cooperation, and closeness—no boundaries, no distance, no restriction.

Looking at our children, we fear that they might feel that their parents do not understand them and do not empathize with them.

Parents who are sensitive toward their children—and most of us are—cannot but identify with them and become overwhelmed with guilt, even when they believe wholeheartedly that educating and setting boundaries are an important part of being a parent.

When a spouse, grandparent, and other people in a child's vicinity also broadcast to a parent that he or she is too hard on the child and too frustrating, feelings of guilt are joined by a sense of loneliness, despair, and depression.

> Galit and Yossi—a psychologist and an engineer—have two children. Danny, their firstborn, is described as quiet, cooperative, and sociable. When Danny was born, Galit stayed home for a year to care for him, and when he started school, she made a point of being with him every afternoon.
>
> Galit believed in boundaries and had no problem setting them. Yossi, on the other hand, had a soft and yielding nature, and in order to avoid confrontations with his son he did not restrict him at all.
>
> When Danny was three years old, Ronny was born. Danny, who found it hard to relinquish his only-child status, became demanding, angry, disappointed, and miserable. Galit felt responsible for the suffering she was causing her older son and was torn between the desire to fulfill his expectations for attention and the demands of caring for his little brother. Because of her feelings of guilt, she tried to compensate Danny with small gestures of attention and love and made sure to find quality time in which she and her husband were exclusively his. All to no avail.
>
> Yossi, who had always aspired to be a "good" dad, felt that the very birth of their younger son deprived Danny of their affection, and he demanded that Galit be more lenient with their older son. Whenever Galit asked Dan-

ny to take a bath or go to bed, Yossi would undermine and invalidate her.

Gradually Galit sank deeper and deeper into a state of misery and depression. At first she didn't understand why she felt so bad, and it was quite some time before she realized that her melancholy stemmed from the feeling that everyone was condemning her—the pathetic look in Danny's eyes was telling her, "You're a bad mother!" Her feelings of guilt at having brought another child into the world and thus depriving Danny of his only-child status also assured her that she was being "a bad mother," and her husband's critical attitude toward her attempts at setting boundaries for Danny sent the same message.

Yossi and Galit tried marriage counseling, which didn't help. They were on the verge of divorce.

Sara, Galit's cousin, saved the family. She explained to Galit that Danny was confused by the differences of opinion between Yossi and herself, and he didn't know how to act. Was he supposed to take a bath, as his mother had instructed, or should he continue playing, as his dad told him? Was he to go to bed at eight o'clock, as his mother said he should, or at a much later hour, as his dad said he could (2-3)?

Sara explained that Yossi's defensive and sympathetic reactions supported and reinforced the boy's feelings of deprivation. She added that Yossi's behavior communicated to Danny that there were two main characters in his life: the "good" one, his dad, who defended him and never frustrated him, and the "bad" one, who took the form of his irritating mother. Under these circumstances, Danny found it hard to formalize a realistic image of his parents, one that was both beneficial and frustrating (2-4).

Galit was unable to accept what sounded like criticism of her beloved and much-admired husband, but when Sara suggested she ask Yossi for his cooperation in setting boundaries, she agreed to try it. But she was in for a surprise; Yossi refused to cooperate. Setting boundaries, he stated, would contradict his liberal worldview and would severely damage the pleasant and beneficial relationship he had formed with his son.

Galit was furious and, on Sara's advice, she decided to take action. One Friday, in Yossi's presence, she allowed Danny to eat chocolate before lunch. She knew for sure that her husband was firmly against this and, sure enough, Yossi demanded that she go back on her word and forbid Danny to eat the chocolate. "By all means," she said, "you do it." Yossi tried to argue with her, but she stood firm. Yossi, who was left no choice, turned to Danny and forbade him to eat the chocolate before his meal. Danny didn't respond and just went on eating the chocolate. Yossi raised his voice and roared at his son—in vain. In desperation, Yossi turned to Galit again; this time he suggested punishing Danny, who by this time was not only eating the chocolate but also screaming and whining. Galit refused. She suggested that he punish his son by himself and promised to back him up.

> The confrontation between father and son turned into a bitter battle. Yossi threatened Danny with punishment if he didn't stop with this behavior. Danny wasn't impressed and just went on eating the chocolate. Yossi snatched the chocolate from Danny and ordered him to go to his room. Danny refused and Yossi forced him into the room. At this stage, seeing his father as an enemy, Danny did everything he could to annoy him. The struggle for power and control lasted for twenty-four hours. Danny was angry; he shouted and he wept bitter tears. Yossi refused to budge. He kept scolding his son. When the twenty-four hours were over, the boy calmed down and went back to being the happy child he had always been before his brother was born.
>
> Yossi was shocked and exhausted. He looked at his son who, after months of anger and tears, was now playing happily, a big smile on his face. He couldn't believe his eyes. Was it really just a matter of setting boundaries—which he had believed would deeply upset the boy—that had reinstated his smile and joie de vivre? He looked at Galit. Something had obviously changed between them. No longer were they a father and a mother. They had become parents.

When it comes to setting boundaries for children, many parents find themselves, like Galit and Yossi, facing an obstacle-riddled path. Some of these obstacles are absolutely human and consist of solidarity and pangs of guilt. Most of the obstacles, however, are the product of the context in which we live—the zeitgeist.

Setting boundaries for children means being critical and judgmental. It's as if parents are telling their children, "I don't like what you are doing. It's not right." It is no wonder, then, that many children react with anger, shame, and insult to the boundaries set by their parents, since criticism is not an easy thing to deal with. Society also doesn't approve of judgments and considers them to be politically incorrect. Many times we hear comments such as, "You don't need to judge him; just try to understand him."All of this makes the setting of boundaries doubly hard.

When society does not clearly delineate the boundaries between what is permitted and what is forbidden, and when those in charge of education recommend the relaxing of boundaries in order to make life easier for children and to allow them greater freedom, it is no wonder that parents are filled with doubts and concerns. Parents' reluctance to impose prohibitions on their children sometimes reaches absurd proportions, especially when parents make decisions that contradict all traces of natural parental instinct. They fail to demand that their children fasten their seat belts when in the car, or avoid fire; they don't insist that their children wear helmets while riding motorcycles or drive their cars at a normal speed.

In June 2002, *Yedioth Aharonot*, an Israeli newspaper, published an article about a fourteen-year-old boy who was caught driving his father's car well over the speed limit on a busy road. The father, who was in the car with him, explained to the arresting officer that he allowed his son to drive the family car because he couldn't cope with the pressure the boy was putting on him.

Chapter Three

Internalizing Boundaries Prepares One For Life

"Why shouldn't she be allowed to smash all her toys? They're hers, aren't they?"

"Why should he be punished for snatching toys from other kids? You don't want the kid to turn into a neurotic wimp, do you?"

"Why does she have to be polite to adults? We're all equal, aren't we?"

"Let's speak to him at eye level."

All these expressions are in the spirit of the zeitgeist, and the fruits they bear are rotten.

Too often, one gets the impression that parents are completely unaware of the fact that they are actually allowed to make demands of their children. We don't mean big demands, heaven forbid, but the kind that in the not-too-distant past were taken for granted, such as to behave "nicely," to sit quietly, to help around the house, to be polite, to speak softly and not yell "I'm entitled," as is so commonplace these days.

The results are children who behave in an abominable manner and parents who do nothing to stop them.

These are the comments of Tel Aviv columnist Eli Mohar, with regard to the failure of education in Israel and the uninspiring achievements of Israeli school children.

Mohar also wrote that "good intentions, like defending children's rights and avoiding punishment, as well as the complete undermining of authority, are what have led to the rise in insolence and violence among children."

Our ultimate inspiration, Sigmund Freud, wrote that "no society can exist reasonably if its individuals do not adhere to boundaries and moral demands" (3-1).

And what about children who refuse to accept authority, who are insolent and disruptive in school, and those who don't wait in line and push others, or express their anger by lashing out and running wild?

It's no fun being a child with no boundaries. He might enjoy a feeling of power, but this is soon replaced by a strong sense of loneliness and pain. His classmates won't want to play with him because he hits them and snatches things from them. Teachers won't like him because it's hard to like a kid who is disruptive, wild, and disrespectful. Regular school frameworks will exclude such a child, who will, sooner or later, experience loneliness and rejection.

All the warmth, acceptance, and forgiveness children receive from their families can't replace a sense of self-worth and belonging that success and real friends provide.

> Dalia, a mother of two, sought treatment for her depression. It was soon revealed that her depression was the result of the deep concern she had for her seven-year-old

firstborn son, Zaki. Zaki often made her feel furious and helpless, but also deeply concerned and sympathetic.

Dalia would get angry when Zaki harassed his little brother, Yair. Since she believed in a gentle and forgiving style of parenting, she focused her efforts on talks with her son in an attempt to help him understand the reason for his behavior. The talks led to no change in Zaki's behavior and Dalia's helplessness intensified. At school, Zaki, who became accustomed to paying no attention to the demands of adults, ignored everything his teacher said and made a habit of lashing out at weaker children in his class. The teacher responded with anger and revulsion. Zaki was hurt. One morning he woke up and refused to go to school, and told his mom that his teacher didn't like him. The mother, who identified with her son's feelings of pain and rejection, hurried to the school, sat down with the teacher, and explained to her that Zaki needed to be accepted, understood, and accommodated. She ignored her own feelings of anger and resentment toward her son for harassing his younger brother and disregarding her instructions. As a mother, Dalia was already highly charged with guilt and sympathy, and she was unable to understand that so long as Zaki did not change his behavior, people would find it difficult to like him. When Zaki started first grade, all the familiar problems from preschool surfaced. He beat other children, pushed them, and snatched away their belongings. The principal's response was swift. She proposed to expel him from the school, which only confirmed his feelings of not being wanted, not being loved, and not belonging.

Dalia continued to suffer on her son's behalf, and only with the help of a therapist did she understand that she would have to change direction. Zaki was not in need of her sympathy—he needed boundaries!

Zaki is not the only kid who, in the absence of parental boundaries, is left unprepared and unable to cope with diverse frameworks. Many children, especially those who have stormy temperaments and are impulsive, find it hard to cope with frameworks and react to every frustration, however small, in a particularly intense emotional manner.

School is one of the first frameworks a child has to contend with, and it is often fraught with frustrations. The necessity to accept the teacher's authority, meet educational requirements, belong to a group, as well as to sit in a classroom and be obliged to do homework, all depend on the ability to delay gratification and endure boredom. A teacher's comments can cause recoil or anger, and social interactions are often a source of envy and insult.

Who is going to prepare the child for the frustrations awaiting him in school?

Can his parents do it?

How is it done? Do we need special psychological tools?

Not at all!

This is not a particularly complicated mission but rather an everyday task that parents can carry out in a very good way.

So long as parents set boundaries for their children's anger and stop them from doing whatever they feel like doing, they help them endure boredom and tolerate frustration.

Every time a parent forces his child to wait in line, to cooperate, and not to attack, he improves the child's social skills.

Children who have had boundaries set for them at home enter school when they are mature enough to deal with the frustrations and disappointments aroused by such frameworks and they are able to integrate successfully. They are liked by their peers and feel wanted and loved. On the other hand, when boundaries are unclear at home, children exhibit difficulties in adapting to a framework and feel rejected and unpopular.

Studies carried out by clinical and developmental psychologist Diana Baumrind show that authoritative parents who set boundaries for their children and punished them, along with being warm and close to them (acts that are not at all mutually exclusive), raised happy children who possess an excellent ability to cooperate with their peers and integrate well into social frameworks (3-2).

Every framework, whether social or professional, introduces us to frustrations, so it is not surprising that behavioral problems in school indicate future problems both in the workplace and in close interpersonal relations (3-3).

Common sense teaches us that a child who is raised in a bubble, exposed only to experiences that are soft, loving, and pleasant, will be unable to withstand the frustrations that reality has in store for him throughout the rest of his life. On the other hand, a child who has tasted boundaries and who has had to cope with frustration and disappointment and the anger that these feelings arouse will, as an adult, find it much easier to overcome hardships and crises.

Boundaries set for a child will prevent her from developing a sense of entitlement; instead, she will have the ability to form firm and long-lasting ties with other people. These ties, by their nature, commonly arouse feelings of frustration and disappointment that must be navigated. Moreover, a child who understands boundaries will be sensitive to the whims of her peers and will often develop assertiveness and the ability to thwart her own whims. The long-term relationships that she will form during the course of her life are based on the awareness that even love and acceptance have their limitations (3-4).

Some parents might claim that a framework isn't everything and that there are plenty of people who have achieved success and happiness without having had one. Others will admit that all their lives they wished they had had the license to do as they wished and would like to grant their children the freedom they themselves had always dreamed of and never had.

These parents who wish they could grant their children a liberal childhood and an unrestricted adolescence might forget that even a sparrow doesn't live a life of leisure; even when it appears to be flying freely in the sky, it is always directing itself toward some objective.

Some parents ignore the fact that school does not necessarily constitute a narrow, boring, restrictive, and irritating framework. The educational challenges it presents and the social frameworks it provides can offer a child a sense of self-respect and satisfaction.

When a youth has dropped out of an educational framework, he will eventually have to find new friends and new interests; otherwise, he might sink into boredom, emptiness, and grow to feel worthless, insignificant, and depressed. Also, the professional future he dreams of, like every child does, becomes obscure and unobtainable.

Eighteen-year-old Or was raised by liberal and permissive parents. They didn't fight him when he refused to go to school, and said nothing when he finally dropped out. Subsequently, despite years of psychological therapy, Or never managed to reenter an educational framework. While his peers graduated from high school and were about to join the army as most teenagers in Israel do, he was working a dead-end job and had no clear plans for the future. Or's parents realized that his therapy had failed and chose a different therapist who took a completely different approach. She focused on setting boundaries for Or, and during their therapy sessions she spoke to him sternly, albeit with much concern. She insisted that he begin to play an active role in his life by carrying out tasks that he had previously shirked completely, such as cleaning his room and washing dishes. While being critical of Or and making demands of him, she was also impressed by his progress and gave him credit for it. The therapy focused on Or's parents' liberal and permissive attitude and the effects it had on his readiness to overcome frustration. During the course of his therapy, Or was eventually able to successfully integrate into an educational framework and got himself a real job, both of which gave him reasons to be proud of his ability to cope. He also began to make plans for the future, which was no longer obscure or unrealistic. He enjoyed a feeling of satisfaction, pride, and hope (3-5).

As his therapy progressed, another change occurred. Or felt he could now withstand temptations and was facing moral dilemmas of a kind he had never experienced before. He felt satisfied with his way of coping and his self-esteem rose whenever he chose to behave in a moral manner.

Contrary to common belief, boundaries do not crush a child's inner world, nor do they restrict her spiritual development. On the contrary! Boundaries, which represent parental expectations and values, help enrich a child's inner world with hopes and aspirations, conflicts and fantasies (3-6) The emotional lives of youngsters who grow up without boundaries or demands are empty and controlled by feelings of desolation and dreariness. Where there is no commitment, there are no dreams of liberty or revolt.

In his book, *A Dispirited Rebellion*, writer Gadi Taub (3-7) refers to the feelings of emptiness and monotony among youngsters growing up in a permissive society. According to Taub, the exhilarating possibility of revolt is denied these young people. In a situation where a child is liberated from the onset, says Taub, there is nothing for the child to be freed from and he misses out on an experience that is wonderful.

In such a society, says Taub, youngsters who seek a liberating experience might well cross the line into regions that are extreme and dangerous.

In the past, young people enjoyed a feeling of freedom and revolt when they smoked cigarettes, or shook off the chains of religion; today, it seems that a sense of freedom is often associated with dangerous drugs or a life of crime.

No limits on animal instincts and no room for fantasy leads to sad and dangerous lives for today's youngsters.

Chapter Four

Understand, Accept, and Forgive: Is This What Helps Your Child?

Dad witnesses his kid hitting another kid and responds by hugging her and asking, "What happened? Why are you angry? Who made you mad?"

Mom gets a beating from her young son and in a gentle voice she says to him, "You are really angry. But I don't like it when you hit me."

Parents allow their kids to spend time with them and with their adult friends until late at night, because they "understand" how "hard" it is for children to leave the grownups and go to their room.

Parents tell their child that they understand how hard it is for him to become accustomed to a school framework and the teachers' demands; they allow the child to stay home from school, or even to leave school altogether.

You could say, "Well, these are empathetic responses that express an understanding of the child's feelings."

But the trouble is that a child interprets his parents' understanding and forgiving empathy as justification for his unacceptable and damaging behavior, even if his parents did not mean for their empathy to be interpreted this way.

Most adults intend to pass on a positive message to their children. Nevertheless, children tend to misinterpret it. For instance, we witness parents talking to their aggressive children in a very polite way, gently explaining that violence is not the answer, and the children pay no attention! They just go on being aggressive.

When a parent hugs a child who has just hurt her brother very badly, and asks her gently, "What did he do to make you react like that?" there is no doubt about the parent's genuine desire to understand the child and help her realize the motives for her behavior. But how does the injured brother feel, or other children in the vicinity, in face of the adult's soft reaction? When violence and contempt are reinforced with such empathy, why would a violent child want to control her impulses?

On the other hand, a parent who sets clear boundaries and punishes his child for her violent behavior sends a clear message that violence will not be tolerated and that it should stop right away.

By nature, a child is desperate for boundaries and thrives when given a code of behavior that can guide him through life. He needs his parents to introduce order into his life and this need is no less important than his need for acceptance and empathy. Indeed, it is an existential need.

According to Dr. James Masterson, a world-renowned psychologist in the field of adolescent psychology, parents' reluctance to set boundaries for their children is perceived by children as negligence and indifference. In Masterson's book *Treatment of the Borderline Adolescents: A Developmental Approach* (4-1), he presents examples of young people who dropped out of educational frameworks and fell into lives of crime. They describe in an offhand tone that their parents didn't dare set boundaries and accepted their uncontrolled behavior with understanding. These youths saw themselves as winners, but according to Masterson, this is no more than a cover-up for their profound sense of emotional neglect. By failing to set boundaries for their children, parents are passing on a message of weakness, and children in turn feel that they cannot rely on their parents' support. As a result, a child's inner serenity is undermined and she finds it difficult to focus her energies on positive creativity.

And indeed, if we only tried to consider the extent of uncertainty a small child experiences when he sets out to face the world, we may understand that setting boundaries is critical (positive as well as negative). Boundaries create a kind of map that helps a child judge his environment and make his own choice about what kind of behavior he should adopt. As he grows older he can move away from the confines of his "map," but the mere existence of this guidance provides him with a firm base and a sense of security.

Chapter Five

Aggression, Fear, and Guilt

A child takes out his anger on everything around him. He strikes out, curses, causes a disturbance, and destroys everything in sight. When his parents refrain from controlling him, whether out of feelings of guilt or because they are afraid he might be "suppressed," or "break," they are harming him.

Once the burden of anger is emptied and a child's pain and frustration dull, he does indeed feel some momentary relief, but he soon develops new feelings that are much more complex. He feels he has been "bad" and becomes afraid of revenge and the loss of love of the people he hurt. Worst of all, his self-love is damaged. He develops anxieties that increase in intensity and he is drawn into a hell of feelings of guilt and paranoia.

Already in 1927 Freud observed that when someone hurts someone else, he may develop a fear that that someone else will eventually hurt him back (5-1). And indeed, it often appears that anxiety and aggression share the same living quarters.

Aggressive children translate their anxieties into paralyzing fears: fear of the dark, fear of monsters, fear of elevators and cockroaches, and so on. To such children, the world is a threatening place that is full of aggression, just as they experience themselves expressing aggression and threatening others.

In many other instances, the reason for anxiety is guilt.

When guilt is accompanied by punishment, the account is closed, so to speak, but when the guilty child is not punished for her actions because she is "understood" and "accepted" by her parents, the feelings of guilt and the expectation to be punished start festering inside. Since she has not been punished before, the child is unable to pluck realistic examples of punishment from her own experience and therefore cannot say to herself, "They'll take my toy away," or, "My parents won't take me to the zoo." Where there is no recollection of punishment, the child can only imagine it, and fantasy is far more frightening than reality.

> Eighteen-year-old Doron sought treatment for anxiety so severe that it was paralyzing him. In the course of his therapy, it emerged that Doron, who had been brought up by liberal and enabling parents, had no respect for any accepted norms, and consistently did whatever he felt like doing. He was forever making demands, teasing, and insulting. His parents did nothing to stop him. They thought that it was important for him to express himself and that he should do whatever suited him. Ostensibly, Doron was an easygoing, happy-go-lucky young man with no reservations about expressing his wishes and his feelings—but this wasn't actually the case. Doron

was not happy. He often experienced himself as being "bad" and didn't know why. When he finally came to the conclusion that there was something wrong with him, he turned to therapy. The psychologist he saw did not make him feel better, so he tried a different one, who very soon concluded that Doron was overwhelmed with feelings of guilt and anxiety and forever under the impression that he would soon be held to account for his acts. Doron felt he deserved punishment and was obsessed by the thought that something bad was going to happen to him. In order to avoid the imminent catastrophe, he started acting out magical thinking. He became very conscious of his behavior. For instance, he was sure that the kind of pants he wore, the street he chose, or the knife with which he buttered his bread would determine whether or not the catastrophe would happen. His obsessive thoughts grew in intensity and there was no sign of any relief.

His therapist explained to him the meaning behind his behavior and suggested that he try acting in a considerate and ethical way toward his peers. She told him that if he followed her suggestion, his feelings of guilt would lessen and so would his anxiety. This line of therapy did indeed lead to a significant reduction in Doron's anxiety levels and to a marked improvement in his obsessions.

Anna Freud, daughter of the founding father of psychoanalysis and a child psychoanalyst herself, refers to similar instances of emotional complexity in her book *The Ego and Mechanisms of Defense* (5-2). According to her, for a long time professionals believed that parental permissiveness and forgiveness toward children would prevent the development of emotional symptoms, since children would then not need to repress their inherent aggressive urges and would therefore not develop inhibitions. Over time, however, it became clear to her that growing up in the presence of softhearted, forgiving parents did not prevent anxieties but actually increased them. According to Freud's interpretation, such children developed anxieties because they were never exposed to restriction sufficient to contain the stormy passions that flooded them.

According to Donald Woods Winnicott, one of the most important psychoanalysts of the twentieth century, a stern parent and reasonable punishment can alleviate the anxiety that results from the fantasy of sadistic revenge that is typical of children's undeveloped superego. This wish for revenge creates sadistic fantasies, similar to those found in nightmares, in children's fears, and in fairytales. Reasonable punishment can serve to reduce children's anxiety (5-3). Winnicott regards parental punishment as neither guilt inducing nor cruel, but rather as an effective replacement for fantasies of revenge that children's undeveloped conscience creates.

Winnicott illustrates this idea in his story of Henry, a forty-year-old married man (ibid., 455–693), who was afraid of experiencing feelings of power. According to Winnicott, Henry's emotional inhibitions were the result of his father's "mollycoddling" him as a child. His father was gentle, forgiving, and understanding, and refrained from punishing him even when Henry behaved aggressively toward his parents. As a child, Henry felt he deserved to be punished and when nothing happened, he learned to restrict his emotions, as a way of restricting his aggressive behavior. In the absence of punishment that would have modified and nullified the boy's aggressive urges and behavior, Henry unconsciously chose to refrain from feeling altogether. Winnicott goes on to say that had the father adopted a paternal stance and set boundaries for his son's behavior, Henry would not have had to restrict his feelings.

According to this concept, the source of feelings of guilt is the actual aggression rather than punishment and other forms of educational means. Moreover, when punishment is part of an ongoing process of boundary setting, it allows children to internalize those boundaries instead and avoid feelings of guilt.

A similar concept is described in the writing of Edith Jacobson, a well-known twentieth-century psychoanalyst. She too believes that setting boundaries could prevent children from having feelings of guilt (5-4).

Chapter Six

Punishment

Why is it necessary to punish?

Why isn't it enough to discuss things? To explain things?

By nature, the setting of boundaries is the opposite of a child's immediate wishes. A child wants to run without restraint and is not concerned with the dangers of a busy road. He lashes out when he is annoyed and this gives him a pleasant feeling of power and release. He wants to watch TV and stay up late. He doesn't want to do his homework. He follows his need for pleasure and is motivated by momentary urges and immediate satisfaction. The stormier his temperament, the greater his tendency to rebel. Thus, when it is time for parents to set boundaries for a child, it is not enough to say no to him, or to offer him explanations, or to make demands of him, because he will simply ignore them.

What, then, will work?

Is punishment the answer?

The issue of punishment is worth explaining.

Punishment is an ancient means of education, which nowadays is avoided like the plague.

Punishment makes a child feel uncomfortable. It drives home to him that there is a price for ignoring his parents' demands.

A smack on the wrist or on the behind, punishments that were commonplace among previous generations, are not only unacceptable today but also illegal, even though punishment itself has lost none of its value. What about punishing a child by withholding her rights to an allowance, toys, sweets, watching TV, and using the computer? Are these modes of punishing more acceptable? And how should we relate to a child's age and personality? Should the type of punishment, its frequency, and its intensity be adapted to the child? The answer is definitely yes.

And what about explanation? Should it be avoided?

In recent years, scientific research has confirmed that in order to set boundaries it is impossible to make do merely with words and explaining. Indeed, studies show that a significant percentage of children do not respond to explanations, requests, or even demands, and only punishment can bring about a change in their unacceptable behavior (6-1).

According to a series of research studies (6-2) that deal with the effectiveness of treatment of violent behavior among kindergarteners, verbal demands were of no use whatsoever and children improved their behavior only after being punished.

What is the value of punishment? Why is it so useful in achieving a change of behavior among children?

In the course of children's everyday life, they need to be exposed to resources that are concrete and tangible, because their overall experience is based to a great extent on the activity and experience absorbed by their senses.

It is inconceivable that children could experience their environment as concerned and loving without them being touched, cuddled, or fed. In the same way, it is impossible for them to be aware of boundaries in the absence of elements that are physical and tangible, like an angry tone of voice, or different modes of punishment that neutralize their strong impulses.

Chapter Seven

When Parents Are Afraid to Punish

Is it possible to raise a child without using punishment or other measures of discipline? Many people have made the mistake of believing that it can be done, and Bertrand Russell practiced this premise with his own children and others in the school he established in 1927. The school closed down five years later and some of Russell's offspring ended their lives tragically in mental hospitals. Nonetheless, even today there are many good people among us who choose to stick their heads in the sand in the belief that education without punishment is possible and even desirable.

Many parents who avoid setting boundaries for their children and refrain from punishing them—whether due to liberal ideals or social pressures—subsequently report feelings of resentment, anger, disappointment, and helplessness in the face of their children's aggressive or disrespectful behavior.

When these feelings of anger are held inside for any length of time, parents are liable to explode in a frightening outburst of shouting, insults, violence, and threats.

The research of Diana Baumrind has shown that most cases of physical outbursts by parents against their children occur among those permissive parents who decide from the beginning to refrain from punishing their children. According to Baumrind, these parents experience pent-up feelings of anger and helplessness and these in turn lead to their outbursts (ibid., 35).

> Jane and Donny are the parents of Josef and Dan. Since a very young age, Jane dreamed she would be a patient and understanding mom, and when she became a mother, she did her very best to live up to her dream, even when her children's behavior infuriated her. Jane's children were very temperamental. Josef, the elder son, tended to burst into a deafening screech that caused unbearable tension all around him; Dan, the younger son, also had a stormy temperament and was physically violent. His violence and unwillingness to accept authority were so pronounced that by the age of three he was expelled from two nursery schools and any social gathering in his presence soon turned into a nightmare.
>
> The parents turned to one-on-one therapy, family counseling, and "play therapy." There was no mention of punishment.
>
> This kind of therapy suited Jane, since she never punished her children and never allowed her husband to punish them. When Dan behaved in an insufferable or dangerous way, she would talk to him and try to understand what his motives were; she also explained to him how he should behave. When his peers distanced themselves from him and rejected him, she used to say, "Please, Danny, just look at what's happened as a result of your behavior. You really should take responsibility for it." Once, as the family was eating their evening

meal, Dan started screeching, threw his plate of food to the floor, and kicked his father. Jane completely lost it. She stood up and dragged Dan to his room. All the anger and frustration that she had restrained for so long came pouring out of her all at once and she gave her son a furious beating. Her fury subsided only after Dan had cried and begged her to stop. This wasn't just a smack on the behind, but a serious, indiscriminate beating. Both mother and son continued to be shocked, horrified, and scarred by the traumatic event.

What about rewards?

Emma and David were married later in life. For as long as she could remember, Emma had dreamed of having a large family and she was in a hurry to have her first baby. The couple had three daughters. Dina, the eldest, and Sheri, the youngest, were smiling, talkative girls, whereas Noa, the middle daughter, suffered from language difficulties and fine motor dysfunction. While Dina and Sheri were lovable and popular with everyone, Noa was always hanging back. She was an angry and grumpy child, lashed out at other children, and suffered from social rejection. Her parents, who found it hard to accept their middle daughter's clumsy movement and stilted language, were also hounded by feelings of guilt and pity. Out of a need to compensate Noa and mollify her, her mother refrained from setting any kinds of boundaries for her. Even the girl's kindergarten teacher avoided setting boundaries and tried the reward system used in formal education. This system was also tried out at home. "If you don't hit anyone today, you'll get ice cream," her mother said. And her father added, "If you agree to wash yourself, I'll read you two stories at bedtime." When Noa wanted to get her reward, she was able to control her behavior, but as soon as she won it, she went back to hitting and harassing everyone in sight. The rewards didn't turn Noa into a happy child. She remained the same miserable and aggressive child she'd always been.

What most impressed the therapist when she first met the family was that Noa used power to control her environment; however, she explained, it wasn't her own power. It was a false power, granted her by the environment, and the rewards she received only served to reinforce and confirm her false power. Finally, Noa reached a state of complete control over everybody in her environment. There was an urgent need to put an end to this control. The therapist believed that it would be possible to channel the energy that fed the false and destructive power by putting Noa in a position where she could help others and by engaging her in sports. She was quite convinced that this was the way to impart to Noa a sense of meaning and satisfaction.

"Enough with the rewards!" the therapist announced. She made it clear that what Noa needed were boundaries and therapy that focused on her physical and linguistic handicaps. When these were tackled and improved, Noa's self-esteem was boosted and as a result, her behavior underwent a drastic change. And most important, Noa was transformed into a happy and sociable little girl in a very short time.

Why is punishment so vehemently avoided?

Are the psychological theories that have flourished during the last hundred years responsible for this? Have they influenced today's educational approach?

Chapter Eight

What Should We Know?

Contrary to common opinion, most of the leading theorists in the field of psychology-psychoanalysis attach great importance to the development of moral inhibitions and moral values, and pay much attention to the ability to experience empathy and guilt.

The first in the list of theorists is Sigmund Freud, who developed a theory that has at its base inherent drives of aggression and sex. Freud stresses that the level of moral demands made by parents, their ability to punish their children, and the respect children show their parents go a long way toward forming children's moral fiber (8-1). In his later writing, Freud points out that it is essential to control impulses and assigns parents an important role in enhancing the development of moral inhibitions—the superego, as he called it, or what today we refer to as boundaries.

Why, then, did most professionals interpret Freud's theory as permissive and forgiving?

Is it possible that Freud's positive attitude toward moral inhibitions was pushed aside because it came at a relatively late stage in his life, whereas it was his earlier and more original discoveries that attracted the most attention? Was it a description of the inner struggle raging within us between instinctual impulses and moral inhibitions that so fired the imagination of Viennese society? Or was it fear of the possible psychological price demanded by the development of strict moral inhibitions—phobias, panic attacks, hysteria, obsessions, and compulsions—that terrified that conservative society in which these beliefs were prevalent at the time? And if moral inhibitions and feelings of guilt are indeed believed to be responsible for the development of mental illness in children, it's only natural that parents would be drawn to permissive educational theories that soften the moral demands and divest their children of feelings of guilt, especially when these theories allow parents to be good and kind to their children.

Also, let's not forget that Freud formulated his theories during the late nineteenth century and the first decades of the twentieth century, a period during which stringent Prussian education was the order of the day and educational demands were far too strict. Let us also not forget that since those far-off days, society has become much more secular and permissive. Nowadays, the boundaries set by conservative educationalists (like ourselves) are nowhere near those set by the society of a century ago. Today we are completely on the other end of the scale and find ourselves witnessing the devastating results of a lack of moral inhibitions. Thus, not only is the attempt to "heal" children by softening moral demands of them archaic, it is even harmful; moreover, **it also makes no sense.**

The theory put forward by Melanie Klein—a brilliant and innovative psychoanalyst of her time, whose moral development theory had a huge impact on psychological thought and on the approach to child education (8-2)—is also problematic.

Klein overturned the concept of moral development. If before her it was acceptable to think that punishment was educational, Klein claims in her writing that it is actually gentleness, forgiveness, and lack of parental criticism toward children that restricts children's aggression and helps develop their moral behavior. Kleinian theory is complex and difficult to understand. We won't try to untangle its many mysteries and will therefore refer only to its conclusions (see note 8-3 for more details).

Klein draws two magic circles: the "good" and the "bad."

The "bad" magic circle consists of parents who are stern, critical, punishing, and frightening. According to Klein, this kind of family framework produces children who grow up without recognizing their aggression, are unable to control it, and turn it against their peers; they have no reservations about hurting people who frustrate them.

The "good" magic circle contains components of gentleness, understanding, acceptance, and parental forgiveness. According to Klein, these components modify a child's inherent aggressiveness, so that it is no longer conceived as destructive. A child who is raised by gentle parents who practice softness rather than aggression, forgiveness rather than criticism, will, in the future, be able to behave toward her peers with the same measure of gentleness and forgiveness, since this accommodating, tolerant, and gentle attitude modeled by the parents will in time diminish her own aggression. As an adult, the child will relate to her peers as both good and bad. As a result, she will treat them with forgiveness, love them, and aspire to avoid harming them.

The conclusion from this theory is that forgiveness generates inhibitions, while punishment and repression lead to aggression. We are looking at a nice, impressive, and novel theory, but we have to remember that theory is one thing and reality is quite another. In recent decades, after many years of implementation of Klein's theory, both in psychoanalysis and education, reality has begun to rear its head. People have come to realize that the gentler and more permissive the education, the more aggressive and violent its products. A careful study of Klein's writing hints at the fact that she herself realized that there is a gap between her theory and reality and that she may have even been concerned that what she said might stop parents from setting boundaries for their children—which is actually what has happened.

In 1937, Klein wrote, "It is well known that a child who is raised by a mother who floods him with love and expects nothing in return, usually becomes an egotist [...] over pampering on the part of the mother causes a child to feel guilty and does not allow him [...] to develop real empathy for others" (8-4).

Twenty-two years later, in 1959, in her paper "Our Adult World and Its Roots in Infancy" (256–257), Klein returns to this point even more emphatically. According to Klein, allowing children to fully express themselves can have negative results both for the children and their parents. Whereas in the past, children were victims of a strict disciplinary approach on the part of their parents, nowadays parents are liable to become victims of their own children. When a child is overindulged by his parents, he may feel that he has an advantage over them. This makes him feel guilty for exploiting them. On the other hand, restrictions provide him with a sense of security; making him respect his parents is essential in forming a healthy relationship in the family and also in developing respect for others. Klein also warns that while Freud's teachings increased the understanding of problems resulting from the way in which a child is raised, they have often been misinterpreted (ibid.). Although it is true that overly strict discipline reinforces a child's tendency to withdraw, it should be remembered that too much indulgence could be just as damaging.

These comments, which we consider to be of the utmost importance, remained marginal in Klein's theory. In fact, it was the general spirit of the theory that emphasized the negative effects of setting boundaries that brought about the change in tone of modern psychology, rather than more moderate approaches such as those of Jacobson, the psychologist and psychoanalyst who worked extensively with children and parents. Jacobson proposed a theoretical model, which somewhat moderates the Kleinian approach. According to Jacobson, the warm and accepting attitude of parents toward their children up to the age of one year is indeed important in creating the first step in the development of moral values, but later on in life, clear demands and even punishment are of enormous importance on children's way to achieving normal moral development (8-5). But does anyone even remember Jacobson today?

On the other hand, we well remember the contribution of one of Freud's successors, the psychoanalyst Thomas Ogden, who made a strong mark on modern psychological concepts. According to his theory, in the course of his development, a child internalizes both his parents' position toward him and his own position toward his parents (8-6). In other words, if a parent abuses a child, the child will internalize the parent's abusive position as well as his own position as victim. The result is that as an adult, his position is sometimes sadistic and sometimes masochistic.

Ogden's theory had great influence on psychological and educational approaches. Its components were taken at face value and became the gospel truth. From then on, professionals were absolutely convinced that the reason for a child's aggression was the aggression she herself suffered, and anyone who was abused as a child would abuse others. Sayings such as "an abused child will grow up to be an abusive parent" became axiomatic, and over the years it was forgotten that this was merely one of many theoretical explanation. Many writers gave preference to this understanding and chose to ignore the day-to-day reality that clearly reflects the fact that increased violence among children and youths is actually happening in an age when children are brought up in an extremely gentle and permissive way.

Another vitally important contribution to the development of the gentle and empathic approach is that of Heinz Kohut, a proponent of the theory of self. According to Kohut, empathy toward a child and admiration for him are what enable his inherent aggressiveness to turn into creative assertiveness, so that anger and aggression are proof that a child suffered from an absence of empathy and a dearth of admiration. Furthermore, according to Kohut, there is no significance to boundaries when raising a child (8-7). He claims that moral inhibitions are the result of a child's solidarity with his parents and fear of upsetting them.

Gentleness, leniency, no boundaries—this is the crux of the modern psychological concept created in the spirit of Melanie Klein, Ogden, and Kohut.

Chapter Nine

Good Parents Don't Punish Their Children: Modern Attitudes toward Punishment

Democracy, the apple of the eye of modern western society, flies the flag of equality, tolerance, and the right of its weaker members to defense and protection. The flag bearers for children's rights adhere to these same values. But should democracy bring about the invalidation of parental authority? Does democracy mean total freedom for children? Is it possible that in the name of democracy, parents are no longer allowed to say no to their children or to punish them? The belief that punishment is harmful to children has long been a part of our culture. It affects each and every one of us and penetrates our awareness via the movies we see and the books we read. It is a concept that has become a kingpin of modern society and helps form the media's attitudes toward parenting, as well as influencing legislation and courtroom decisions.

In recent years, the children's rights movement has enjoyed enormous momentum and among the current generation, this movement has become pivotal and is stronger than ever before. Educational systems are embracing psychological concepts in which stern approaches and firm discipline during childhood are said to create emotional problems in adulthood, and liberal concepts have become the order of the day.

To prevent parents from abusing their children, the public is constantly being bombarded by messages of clemency and boundless consideration; effectively, children should be forgiven, parents should be understanding, and punishment should be avoided.

Out of a desire to protect children from all hardship and unpleasantness, parental authority has become enfeebled and boundaries have been blurred. Nonetheless, at the same time society has seen a worrying rise in violence, from domestic violence to violence at school and on the streets.

Sweden, a pioneer in enacting legislation that limits parental authority, is now experiencing a dramatic rise in child and youth violence. The country's lawyers and academics, who have established a committee for human rights, are now protesting that while Swedish children are protected against light physical punishment from their parents (e.g., being spanked on the bottom), they are exposed to much more serious violence from their peers. The committee's position is supported by statistics that indicate a dramatic rise in attacks on children and youths by their peers over the years since the law went into effect (9-1).

Is it conceivable, therefore, that a connection exists between legislation that forbids across-the-board physical punishment and a rise in youth violence?

We believe so!

In Israel, where physical punishment has been forbidden since 2000 (9-2), there has also been a steady and sharp rise in youth violence, which bears an obvious connection to reduced parental authority. Children and adults are subjected to vicious beatings and even murder at the hands of violent youths, while parents, who should by nature be responsible for setting boundaries for their children, are denied the right to do so properly, as they are weakened by the authority of the law.

Parents are constantly under suspicion, and the fear that they may act in a punitive manner toward their wayward children has paralyzed them and led to the almost complete transfer of their power into the hands of law-enforcement authorities.

Is this what we had hoped for? Are the indifferent and hesitant law-enforcement authorities a suitable substitute for concerned and caring parents? We are well aware of the fact that law-enforcement authorities are not always able to effectively do their jobs, which, in turn, leads to the crumbling of society.

Chapter Ten

Spanking?

Spanking? Heaven forbid!

Still, the public should be made aware of a study published in the United States that shows that over 80 percent of parents with children aged between two and six years old reported that they spanked their children on the bottom (Straus and Stewart 1999).

The public should be aware of a poll conducted among hundreds of American pediatricians that reveals that over 50 percent of those polled recommended a spanking on the bottom as a means for instilling discipline (McCormick 1992).

A spanking on the bottom is almost certainly the most spontaneous parental response to bad behavior by toddlers, and we should remember that spontaneous parental responses are usually harmless. A nursing mother who taps her baby on the back when it starts to choke is doing the very best and correct thing, although she never learned it in any first-aid course. A father who returns from work and joyfully lifts his son up in the air is doing exactly what he should be doing, even though he never attended a course on the subject.

Spontaneity is fundamental to any parent-child relationship. Why, then, are we so reluctant to deal an errant child a quick spanking on the bottom? Perhaps it is because the media tends not to make a distinction between a spanking on the bottom and a lash with a belt, and sending a child to his room for a few minutes has become tantamount to imprisonment?

American researchers are divided over the effect corporal punishment can have on children. Some researchers have warned that instructive spanking on the behind has a negative effect on a child and leads to violence, depression, and poor academic achievement (10-1).

Others believe that the picture is altogether more complicated (10-2) and indicate that most researchers have not distinguished between a spanking on the behind and much harsher beatings, such as using a belt, hair pulling, or kicking, which makes it difficult to reach unequivocal conclusions.

Who can tell whether instructive spanking is indeed educational?

Dr. R.E. Larzelere has reviewed a series of studies on this subject and has listed the conditions under which spanking is most definitely educational (10-3).

According to Larzelere, an instructive spanking is one that is dealt by loving, concerned parents and is not in any way brutal, frequent, or the result of loss of control. A spanking has an educational effect when it is given legitimacy by the context of the situation and when it is dealt to a child who is older than two and younger than six who knows exactly why he is being punished. Thus, according to Larzelere, parents who do not believe in instructive spanking are more liable than other parents to lose control and resort to hitting their children.

According to another study, in which Larzelere joined Schneider, Larson, and Pike (10-4), children who were *not* punished by their parents exhibited a severe regression in their behavior. The 1988 study conducted by diLalla, Mitchell, Arthur, and Paglicea came to similar conclusions: Youths who grew up with non-punishing parents who instead made do with talks and explanations, developed a more violent behavioral pattern than youths who had been punished (even beaten) (10-5).

Roberts's research series (ibid.) also show that behaviorally disrupted kindergarteners who were punished with a spanking on their behinds improved in their behavior after punishment. The improvement enabled parents to use milder forms of punishment later on.

In Israel, corporal punishment is forbidden according to the ruling of Supreme Court Justice Beinish (4596/98: Anonymous vs. the State of Israel) and, notwithstanding the fact that this ruling related to an extreme case in which a mother beat her children with undue cruelty, public opinion has adopted a complete ban on all kinds of physical punishment by parents, including instructive spanking dealt by a parent's loving hand. Beinish's ruling aroused furious responses and inspired Judge Evelyn Gordon to write a sharply critical article on the subject(10-6).

The across-the-board ban on corporal punishment, combined with the obligation to report all cases of abuse involving the underage and helpless, while relying on the discretion of welfare authorities, has created a completely absurd situation. Parents are afraid to touch their children, afraid that the children themselves, their neighbors, kindergarten teachers, school teachers, and others will report them to the authorities.

Ruth and Michael, university graduates from northern Israel, got married at a relatively late age and had their first son, Yair, when they were both thirty-four. Yair was hyperactive from a very early age, his motor skills and linguistic development were slow, and he had temper tantrums and suffered from separation anxiety. When he was three years old he was referred for psychiatric evaluation.

The doctor diagnosed impaired fine and gross motor skills, linguistic problems, and high levels of aggression and anxiety. He referred Yair to an occupational therapist and a speech therapist, and instructed the parents to set strict boundaries for their son. The improvement in Yair's behavior was instant and he turned into a happy and popular child, a source of pride and joy for his parents, and an inspiration to his teacher.

When Yair was five years old, his sister was born. The labor was difficult and traumatic, and Ruth was greatly weakened and unable to function properly. Yair underwent a setback, started to wet his bed at night, and exhibited signs of anxiety during the day. In distress, Ruth turned to her mother, a retired teacher, to help her care for the baby. Ruth's mother, a pedantic and determined woman who had severed relations with three of her adult children, took on the task willingly. Soon Ruth and Michael noticed that she had taken control of the entire family. Yair's condition regressed further and his parents, who tried to set boundaries for him, encountered hostile reactions from Ruth's mother. She believed that they were being too harsh on the boy, undermined the boundaries they had set, and compensated Yair with gifts. Yair's bad behavior escalated and his condition became extreme. He cried endlessly, refused to go to kindergarten, and insisted on sleeping with his parents every night.

The situation at home became unbearable. One morning, when Michael was in a hurry to leave for work, Yair refused—as usual—to get out of bed and dress himself. All argument was futile and eventually Michael gave his son a spanking on the behind. Ruth's mother, who was present at the time, jumped up as if bitten by a snake. She made straight for the welfare services and issued a formal complaint, stating that her son-in-law was abusing his son.

The welfare worker assigned to the case used her discretion and turned first to the pediatrician who knew the family and was familiar with Ruth's mother's difficult character. The pediatrician absolutely ruled out any possibility of child abuse, but Ruth's mother would not let go and lodged a complaint with the police. Now a dance of demons had begun and both the parents and their children were drawn into it. The police charged the father with abuse and cameras were installed in Yair's kindergarten to monitor the boy's behavior and to follow any changes in his mood. The parents were told that they were under constant surveillance and were forbidden to touch their son.

The parents were miserable. They felt that their child had been taken away from them and, even worse, they felt that their son had lost his parents, as their authority had been wiped out. The absurdity reached a peak when, one afternoon, Michael and Yair went for a walk in the park. When it became dark, Michael told his son that it was time to go home. Yair refused and Michael was faced with a difficult dilemma. Under normal circumstances, he wouldn't have hesitated to hoist the boy up into his arms and carry him home. But in the current, tenuous situation, he was anxious about touching the boy for fear of being reported to the police. He stayed with the child in the park until midnight, when the exhausted Yair fell asleep. What a horror story! And all because of a spanking on the behind!

We are not trying to recommend spanking a child on the behind, or indeed inflicting any kind of corporal punishment! This is not the objective of this book. Our objective is to make the public aware of the various opinions available in western culture on the issue of punishment in general and corporal punishment in particular.

It is important to also stress the importance of parents becoming aware of their children's reactions to punishment. Does punishment put an end to the child's aggression? Does it encourage aggression? Is the parent's choice of punishment too harsh? Does it frighten the child? Each individual parent should be able to recognize his own child's response.

"Train up a child in the way he should go: and when he is old, he will not depart from it" (Proverbs 22:6).

And one final word of wisdom: We as parents are not to blame, as we are raising the apple of our eye. Children are not to blame if we do not stop them. We, as grown-up professional, rational people and as members of a society that needs to exist and propagate, bear the responsibility to discipline our children for the sake of our survival.

Chapter Eleven

Punishment: A Dirty Word, or Necessary for a Child's Development?

Those who oppose corporal punishment believe that the very use of force passes on a counter-educational message that teaches children that strong people are allowed to use force in order to get to those who are weaker than themselves. We don't agree! **Children need their parents to be strong!** It gives them a sense of security and reduces their anxiety.

> Five-year-old Nadav was tall and strong compared to his peers. His physical strength enabled him to easily obtain everything he wanted. When he wanted to go down the slide, he simply pushed aside the other children who were standing in line waiting their turn. When he fancied a toy, he simply grabbed it out of the hands of whoever was playing with it. When he became annoyed in kindergarten, he lashed out at the other children, and when his parents demanded that he take a bath

or go to bed, he ignored them. At family gatherings he made a habit of pestering everyone in his vicinity. His parents, devoted, loving, and decent, were ashamed of their son's unruly behavior. They told him, "No," and, "Don't." They said, "If you go on doing that, we'll have to take you home." They even carried out their threat, but Nadav would not stop. He kept doing whatever he did simply because he could! His parents, who feared that because of their son's deviant behavior he would be put in a "special needs" kindergarten, sought advice, and it was soon revealed that Nadav was not receiving any kind of punishment, and that he was a very anxious and insecure child. Indeed, his parents were afraid that punishment would break his spirit. The therapist explained that this was not the way to do things and that for the sake of Nadav's future their approach had to change. The father then took matters into his own hands and became decisive and constant; he was backed by his wife and no longer hesitated to punish his child. At first Nadav cried and ranted when he was sent to his room, or when a toy was taken from him, but after only a few days of conflict, matters underwent a drastic change and Nadav stopped his aggressive behavior. To the surprise of his parents, he in no way became a sniveling wreck. He had lost none of his former zeal, except that now it was serving him in positive ways.

By instilling boundaries, the family reinstated its sanity, and the "inverted hierarchy" that allowed Nadav to tyrannize his parents (11-1) now made way for a correct and natural hierarchical structure and for genuine closeness between parents and children.

Nowadays, punishment has become a dirty word, but the fact is that when adults refrain from talking to a child in the language of punishment, they are denying her access to the real world.

When a parent or a teacher chooses to say, "Go and calm down in your room," instead of saying, "You are going to your room as punishment for what you have done," they are denying the real meaning of the situation—"I am being punished for what I have done"—and presenting a twisted reality that says, "You are agitated and we are not angry with you; we are not criticizing you and don't believe that you should be punished. We are only concerned for your welfare."

When parents insist on addressing their child in a soft and tender voice, stroking and embracing her even when they are furious with her, how can she trust them? When anger is denied and negative feelings are presented in a positive light, and when body language and words are not on a par with real feelings, how is a child supposed to interpret reality?

How can she tell if smiles, caresses, and appeasing words are expressions of affection or just a smokescreen for anger and disapproval?

Chapter Twelve

Arm Wrestling: Who Is Stronger?

What are our children concerned with? What troubles them? What are they afraid of and what causes them suffering?

The answers to these questions should determine, to a large extent, our attitude toward our children.

According to accepted psychological concepts, throughout their childhood and adolescence children often concern themselves with questions such as, "Will my parents love me as I am?" and, "Are they proud of me?"

It is with this in mind, therefore, that we are reluctant to punish, or to react to our children with anger and disapproval; we are simply afraid of causing them to feel that we don't love them or that we are not proud of them.

When parents are aware of their own feelings, they realize that their emotional reactions to their children change in accordance with their children's age. A baby crying in his crib or a toddler holding out a chubby hand to pull at his mother's hair arouse feelings that are completely different than those aroused by a six-year-old throwing herself down on the floor in a tantrum when she doesn't get what she wants.

We feel intuitively that our helpless little baby needs total acceptance, whereas our older, more independent child, who is getting stronger and stronger and can now run and talk and touch things he shouldn't, arouses in us the need to restrict him.

It is at this age that conflicts begin with regard to everyday activity such as taking a bath, brushing teeth, putting away toys, going to bed, etc. It becomes necessary to use a lot of "no's" in order to prevent physical violence, running into the street, and misbehaving. Relationships between parents and children are constantly undergoing change.

No longer is it a case of absolute sacrifice. Altruism makes way for a reality in which conflicts of interest and discord reign.

The struggle begins and is soon joined by a series of new feelings: battle rage, the joy of victory, the guilt of victory, and the pain of defeat and surrender (12-1).

At the same time, power struggles herald the dramatic change that takes place in a child's play patterns. Ball games, toys, and tumbling blocks gradually disappear and are replaced by war games: swords, guns, Power Rangers, Superman, and Batman. The most exciting gifts a child can receive at that stage are no longer garbage trucks or cement mixers, but swords, shields, and toy soldiers. Favorite TV shows are now those that feature superheroes, conquerors, and conquered. A child is very involved in issues of power and lack of power and tests his strength and his limitations, both through play and his relationship with his parents in real life.

Most parents would have willingly done without the struggles; they would have happily adopted the role of good, kind, and beneficial parents. When they decide to have children, parents never imagine that war, victory, and defeat will become an integral part of their relationship with their children.

"If setting boundaries causes our son to experience surrender and defeat, maybe we should avoid it? After all, we don't want him to feel crushed."

It's true. A child experiences boundaries as defeat. He feels that his parent is stronger than him. At the present stage in his development, he is unable to experience things any differently. From where he stands, the world is divided between the strong and the weak and between victory and defeat.

Will this defeat be forever carved into his awareness?

We believe that this is a stage along the way to more balanced experiences.

We also believe that sidestepping power struggles at this stage in a child's development is tantamount to ignoring his need to test his own strength vis-à-vis that of his parents and, especially, his parents' strength against his own. In the absence of such a test, a child remains with no answers to questions that are of concern to him:

Am I strong?

Am I weak?

Are you, Mom and Dad, going to be able to restrict me? Will I be able to lean on you?

Who's going to win, me or you?

Who's going to have control—will it be me over you, or you over me?

Am I pathetic? Am I a hero?

And finally: Isn't the real world defined by the division between the strong and the weak?

You might say, "Well, a parent's strength is not measured in physical terms or by his ability to impose his demands on his child." You might also say, "Actually, a parent's ability to hold back and not impose her will on her kids is the measure of her mental fortitude as a person." Indeed, the ability to hold back and respect others is a measure of mental fortitude, but one shouldn't forget that for the first few years of a child's life, he doesn't see things like that. Children think in a concrete way and, as far as they are concerned, strength is measured by a person's ability to impose his demands on others and not on the ability to give in. The understanding that restraint is the result of emotional strength comes at a later stage in life, when a child has perfected self-control and the ability to conceptualize.

Parents who refrain from restricting their child out of fear of upsetting him are unaware of the fact that from a child's point of view things appear completely different. At this particular stage in his development, the child is much more impressed by strength than by empathy. His parents' gentle words, as well as the explanations and the concessions, are perceived by the child as signs of weakness and vulnerability that invite him to impose his control over them, rather than as testimony to their love for him.

But even as a child controls his parents and rejoices in the sweetness of his victory, there already lurks within him the terrible fear of the pitch darkness of abandonment. Who will be there to protect me? Who will be there to guide me and support me through the dense forest of life?

Chapter Thirteen

The Price of Victory

"If I, as little as I am, can force my parents to surrender, anyone can," says the child to himself, while feeling all alone in a harsh and complex world.

"If my own parents are unable to deal with my aggression and demands, who is going to help me cope?"

The child who has overcome his parents stands exposed and vulnerable facing two fronts: brutal reality and his own inner world, crammed with powerful urges and impulses. His anxiety rises and then intensifies and is interpreted as concrete fears. As a result, we encounter in our clinic children who on the one hand are not afraid of authority, are full of disdain for their parents, and have no respect for boundaries; and on the other hand, they are also haunted by fears and nightmares. They are afraid of the dark, elevators, food, ants, cockroaches, and much more.

It is fascinating to see how such children choose to adhere to, of all people, parents who constantly struggle with them over boundaries, although they are ostensibly less "accommodating." The reasons for this phenomenon are obvious; such parents are perceived by the children as "strong" and "knowledgeable," and as such, provide them with a sense of security.

> Irit and Menahem, parents of two, came for a consultation. Their older son, Hili, refused to attend school. Menahem, a cardiologist, spent a lot of time away from home and as a result, wanted the little time he had for his children to be fun for them all; he wanted to be the "good" dad. When their dad was at home the children were delighted. The word "no" was not to be heard. They were allowed to go to bed late, eat in the living room in front of the TV, and jump on the sofas. They weren't required to lift a finger to tidy their room. When Irit tried to restrain them and make some demands of them, Menahem would stop her and ask her to let go.
>
> Hili developed an anxiety that steadily increased and, despite the anger he expressed toward his mother, he used to follow her everywhere, refusing to be separated from her. His irritability increased and when he started his first year of school the situation became acute. Every morning he would burst into tears and beg to be allowed to stay at home and, when he arrived at school, he would ask to be let out of the classroom to call his mother. He was unable to concentrate on his schoolwork and his teacher suggested the family seek professional advice.
>
> A therapist suggested that the problem lay with the father's permissive attitude. Menahem was extremely surprised; after all, he had invested considerable effort in

making his time with the children as pleasant as possible, and could hardly imagine that his permissiveness and lack of boundaries would cause the children to feel anxious. Nonetheless, he accepted the opinion of the therapist, who suggested he support his wife's approach and forbid Hili from calling his mother more than once a day from school. After only two or three days, Hili had completely stopped calling his mother. His concentration improved significantly and he appeared happy and liberated. He had managed to let go of his mother's apron strings and started visiting his school friends in their homes. Menahem was in for another surprise. Hili, who until then had been remote from him despite Menachem's efforts to be friends with him, became proud of his father and enjoyed their time together.

This story comes as no surprise to us. Experience has taught us that children want to be able to look up to their parents; after all, a father's strength is also his child's strength. If parents are perceived as weak, it arouses in their children feelings of anger, anxiety, disdain, helplessness, and even contempt. Children tend to be ashamed of weak parents and try to dissociate from them.

In Hili's case, the absence of boundaries led to anxiety and introversion. In other cases, the absence of boundaries may lead to aggressive and out-of-control behavior.

Chapter Fourteen

Weak and Strong All in One

Sometimes parents can encounter passionate reactions when they attempt to set boundaries for their children. Tears, rage, shouting, and violence are fairly common responses and the more difficult the temperament of a child, the stormier her reaction will be.

At the beginning of boundary setting, a child's transition from strength and power to experiences of submission and weakness is sharp, and is liable to arouse feelings of confusion and anger, resentment and disappointment, hostility and desperation. Nonetheless, it should be remembered that this constant movement between strength and weakness, and the encounter with these feelings within a loving relationship, train a child to bear them and to become accustomed to the confusing experience of having to alternate between feelings of weakness and strength.

A child who has boundaries set for him learns that he may be weak in certain situations such as not being able to make decisions about important issues in his life, and strong in other situations such as kicking a ball or solving math problems.

The experience of having boundaries set for them introduces children to the principle of reality and teaches them that in order to achieve what they want they must recognize the strength of others and their dependence on them. They learn to recognize the complexity of what it means to attain their will; that they must coax, and negotiate, and will sometimes have to compromise and also cooperate.

In the 1960s, when the Flower Children celebrated liberty, freedom, and the breakdown of boundaries, the British analyst Dr. Masood Khan warned of the dangers inherent in an absence of boundaries. His experience treating adults had taught him that permissive mothers who refrained from expressing anger toward their children and prevented the fathers from challenging them over boundaries raised children who expected to receive constant concessions from their environment, and, when these were denied them, they were filled with disappointment, anger, and were quick to break off all relations with the perpetrators of their disappointment. According to Khan, parental permissiveness and parents' endless acceptance prevented children from processing their inherent aggression. As a result, he stated, his patients suffered in adulthood from attacks of anger and found it hard to turn their aggression into energy. Khan coined the term "insufficient parental assertiveness" (14-1).

> Two-year-old Shiri, a lively and happy child, had a habit of throwing herself down on the floor whenever her parents raised their voice at her, or did not give in to her demands. It appeared that any setting of boundaries separated her immediately from a sense of power and left

her devoid of vitality. It would be several minutes before she recovered and returned to her games. It was not easy to watch that helpless little creature lying prone on the floor, but her parents, following the advice of a therapist, refused to give in and continued setting boundaries. These educational methods bore very good results.

Shiri is now an opinionated, sociable, and strong six-year-old. She behaves in accordance with the boundaries that have been set for her, and at the same time she is still the energetic and the enthusiastic child she has always been.

A fierce reaction to having boundaries set is an expression of an affront to a child's sense of power, as well as an expression of pain, insult, and wounded pride.

Chapter Fifteen

Pride, Insult, and Respect

Pride and insult are two conflicting and extremely powerful feelings.

Every instance of recognition, compliment, and praise feeds a child's sense of pride, while every "no" a child hears, every rejection and criticism, sow the seeds of insult.

Little and dependent as I am, a nobody, unable to control my life, my pride is badly hurt. Being the subject of criticism while my peers are being praised is a big blow to my pride...

Jealousy, anger, and insult choke me.

How can we bear the hurt pride, jealousy, and pain of humiliation? Who will help us control ourselves and stop us from lashing out in anger, in order to rescue our lost honor and prove that we are strong and in control and thus erase the pain?

According to Kohut, a child who is praised by his parents will develop a self-image so positive that even a narcissistic attack on his pride will not cause him to break down (ibid.). Is this indeed the case?

Admittedly, appropriate admiration on the part of a parent provides an important condition to instilling a sense of security in a child, but not good enough to prevent the pain and insult and humiliation aroused by criticism and rejection, nor is it able to stem the furious responses to these affronts.

Many children and adults living among us were fortunate enough to be on the receiving end of flattery, admiration, and love, yet they respond to any affront with harmful aggression.

> Seven-year-old Rani is the oldest son of Hagit and Ori, who are loving, concerned, and supportive parents. Rani is talented and intelligent but totally incapable of dealing with any narcissistic affront, however minor. When his peers don't agree with him, he hits them, and when adults criticize his behavior, he bursts into bitter tears that last for hours. Rani's parents—gentle, liberal-minded people, the dream of every children's rights advocate—talk to him and try to understand his feelings and bring about a change in his behavior, but in vain. Rani does whatever he wants. He knows only two states, being weak or being strong, and he keeps moving between the two, unable to settle on a happy medium.

When a child's inability to contain hurt pride dwells side by side with high levels of aggression and violence, the results can be catastrophic. In December 2001, a daily newspaper in Israel published a story about a thirteen-year-old boy who attacked and seriously wounded a boy his own age, causing him a severe head injury. "He hurt my son's honor," the boy's father explained. "My son is a good kid, but he is easily insulted."

Like pride and honor, jealousy can also drive people wild.

Eighteen-year-old Sana is the fourth daughter in an Israeli Arab family from northern Israel. Her father, a warm, kind, and gentle man, works for a marketing company. He had dropped out of school at an early age to help support his family. His wife, pretty and well educated, works as a teacher at a local high school. Sana's three older sisters are pretty, well dressed, and polite. All three are law school graduates who work in their profession. Two of the older sisters have married into the most distinguished family in their village.

Sana is very different from her sisters. She suffers from acne, is overweight, awkward, and her academic achievements are not impressive. She has been expelled from several schools due to severe behavioral disruptions. When her mother was hospitalized after a car accident, Sana's behavior worsened. She was frequently absent from home, became involved with children her parents disapproved of, dressed in a provocative way, and became verbally and physically abusive toward her parents.

Sana's relationship with her sisters was problematic. She was profoundly jealous of them, often complained of being discriminated against and humiliated, and she was forever aggravating them. When it became known that the third daughter was going to be engaged to a lawyer, the son of a wealthy local family, Sana became even more frustrated. Consumed with jealousy, she started her revenge. A few days before the engagement party, the two families planned to travel to the nearest big city to buy traditional gold jewelry for the bride. Sana initiated a violent quarrel with her sisters and their father, who had just returned from work in order prepare for the happy occasion, tried to separate them. At that very moment, the police arrived, having received information about the incident from Sana's friends. They interrogated everyone in the house, and when Sana accused her father of abusing her, they arrested **him**!

The entire village was in turmoil. The engagement was cancelled. The bride fell into a deep depression and the whole family was ostracized. Their home, which had always been full of guests, was now empty. No one came to visit. Only Sana celebrated her victory.

In the therapist's office, the parents told the family's sad history. At the beginning of the session, the parents seemed to be ashamed and helpless as their daughter tried to control and navigate the narrative, but the therapist soon overturned this distorted hierarchy and the balance of power was reinstated, as was the parents' lost esteem. With this reinforcement, their spines straightened. Sana, to her great consternation, was forced to listen to her parents' version of the story, which she had tried so hard to disguise. For the first time, she heard about her learning difficulties, her frustrations, her jealousy, her hate, and the destruction she had wreaked upon her own family. She didn't like what she heard, but this time she could not escape from reality. She was no longer in control.

Her father mustered all his courage and admitted that for the first time in his life, he had considered appealing to the *qadi*—a religious judge—to enforce Sharia law on his wayward daughter, who had threatened to destroy his family. Sharia law, explained the father, allows parents to dispossess a wayward child of all his inheritance and to deny him the use of the family name. Sana was in shock. She had never imagined that her parents had so much power and that they were also capable of wielding it.

The change took place in the office itself. Sana, who lost her control over the family, control that was now revealed as false, expressed deep regret and the members of the family left the stormy meeting full of renewed hope. The threat worked as if it had actually been put into operation. The parents were very much empowered, and in the course of the treatment, Sana learned to respect them, help them, and be helped by them. She started to look after herself, improved her appearance, invested in skin care, and changed her style. She also enrolled in a new school and, for the first time in her life, she began to experience the pleasure of receiving compliments and the joy of success. Sharia law was no longer relevant.

Chapter Sixteen

Insult Is Not the End of the World

When a parent sets boundaries for his child as part of a close and secure relationship, the child gradually develops an ability to bear having his pride wounded without experiencing an emotional breakdown.

How come? Any boundary has the potential to wound a child's pride.

Pride is wounded because boundaries are interpreted as criticism and as a sign of weakness and dependence, and, when they are set, a child realizes that she is not perfect.

Nonetheless, in a child-parent relationship there are also many moments of closeness and love, admiration and praise. This complex relationship allows a child to build his own positive self-esteem and emotional invincibility and develop a resistance to any future narcissistic injury.

A child's self-esteem is based, among other things, on his ability to practice **control**, either self-control or control over parents and peers. The boundaries set for a child ameliorate his control over parents and peers and allow him to release energy and channel it into developing his skills—physical, academic, and social. Thus the control he is denied on one hand is reinstated on the other, and this time it is more realistic and positive.

Through this process a child is also able to internalize the value of humbleness.

However, if parents are unable to restrain their child for fear of her aggression, this developmental process will not occur.

Some parents who fear their child will have a breakdown if his pride is wounded(16-1) invest all their energy in "defending" him. At home they don't set boundaries for fear of hurting him, and outside the home they fight other figures of authority, such as school teachers, who they suspect are injuring their child's pride.

This kind of parenting is quite common. Unfortunately, in the long run, it may fail the child.

> Sharon is the youngest daughter of older parents. Her father is a computer expert and her mother is a housewife. Unlike her older sisters, Sharon had no demands made of her. She was raised in a wealthy home and was given everything she asked for. She was never punished and her parents were never angry with her. When she was fifteen, she dropped out of school following two years during which her parents turned a blind eye to her increasing absences. Sharon had great ambitions but after leaving school, the jobs she was offered were not compatible with her talents or aspirations. Without a daily schedule, Sharon made a habit of sleeping until the af-

ternoon. At night she found it hard to fall asleep and developed severe anxiety.

Her parents sent her for counseling. Her therapist thought that Sharon's anxiety, as well as her inability to bear frustration, were the result of a lack of boundaries. He instructed the parents to stop giving her money and to demand that she clean her room and shoulder her share of the household chores.

One day, Sharon quarreled with her father after he had refused to give her money to buy clothes. She told the therapist that she shouted at her father and called him derogatory names, to both of their surprise. In a loud voice the therapist rebuked Sharon: "How dare you speak like that to your father? Where do you get the nerve? I forbid you to talk like that to your parents." Sharon was shocked. She had not expected such a passionate response and announced that she would not allow anyone to talk to her like that.

That evening, Sharon's parents called the therapist.

They told her that their daughter arrived home agitated and tearful, telling them that the therapist had insulted her and announced that she was not interested in continuing her therapy. Upon the therapist's advice the parents did not react. The next week, Sharon returned to the therapist and informed her that in the past, she had also tended to get carried away on an emotional joyride and made a habit of severing relations in the wake for any event she conceived as insulting, reproachful, or critical of her. This kind of behavior was especially pronounced at school. Whenever her teachers criticized her, or refrained from complimenting her, she would respond with anger and pain that were so intense and therefore so frightening to her parents that they made no protest when she decided to leave school altogether.

In the course of the therapy, the therapist often frustrated Sharon and instructed her parents to do the same at home. Over time, Sharon's ability to cope with frustration improved and she no longer experienced criticism as an insurmountable obstacle. Eventually she returned to school and experienced success in her studies.

Chapter Seventeen

"Strong and Bad" vs. "Weak and Good"

Dorit and Gadi are the parents of twins. Ever since their birth, the twins had woken up several times every night. The parents were reconciled to this and accepted it with love. When the twins were two years old and nothing had changed, Dorit, who was the one who regularly got up to tend to them, felt that enough was enough. She had accumulated large quantities of sleep deprivation and her job performance was affected. The children were also suffering from sleep deprivation and were tired and grumpy throughout the day. Dorit suggested to Gadi that they stop their habit of getting up every night, but he refused, claiming that it was important to get up to reassure the children whenever they demanded it. The issues of getting up at night in general, and specifically setting boundaries for the children, became a serious bone of contention in the couple's lives. Dorit was in favor of setting boundaries for the twins, whereas Gadi was convinced that this approach would prove damaging and deny them a sense of freedom and liberty.

Dorit and Gadi decided to try relationship counseling. The therapist tended to see things from Gadi's perspective. According to the therapist, the children were waking from their sleep because they were anxious and suggested a solution—allow the children to sleep next to their parents' bed. The already impossible situation became unbearable. Throughout the night the children moved from their bed to their parents' and the couple was exhausted. Their quarrels escalated and they started to discuss separation. Dorit, who was constantly afraid that the family would fall apart, ended the counseling sessions and turned to another kind of therapy.

The new therapist took a completely different approach. Dorit was given a new nighttime routine. She was to go over to one of the twins as soon as he awoke, take him out of his bed, and wake up his sibling. Then she was to give them both a cup of cocoa, turn on the TV and play a DVD, switch on the lights in the house, and behave as if a new day had dawned. After all this, the noise would wake Gadi, who would come to ask what was happening. Dorit was instructed to respond, "When I wake up, the whole house wakes up."

Dorit was hesitant about so drastic a step, but after a few more sleepless nights she decided to give it a try and followed it to the letter. That stormy night Gadi was unable to go back to sleep and remained amazed and furious.

The following night, with the first sounds of crying, Gadi

jumped out of bed and rushed to the children's room. Holding one of them in his arms, he came into the master bedroom and said to the child, "Look, you have a bad mommy! She refuses to get out of bed for you!" Gadi was expressing anger and profound frustration, but his words were also an expression of his real feelings—that by setting boundaries for his children, by refusing to attend to them and thwarting their demands, he was being "bad," whereas constantly caving in to their demands and setting no boundaries made him a "good" parent.

And indeed, from a child's point of view and often, lamentably, from an adult's point of view as well, the struggle over boundaries has two sides. On one side there is a winner and on the other, a loser. The winner is the strong one and is perceived as "bad," and the loser is the weak one and is perceived as "good."

When parents start setting boundaries, children feel themselves to be "strong" and "bad"—they think, "I'll continue to misbehave/lash out/yell/disturb, even if Mom asks me to stop." They think, "I'll make my own decisions and I don't care about anyone else." People observing this see the child as "bad" and feel that she needs to be taught a lesson.

Things change as the struggle for boundaries progresses; children give in to their parents. Now the child thinks, "My parents are strong and bad. They are hurting me. I am the good guy here." At the same time the observers undergo a change. Now they identify with the child, feeling sorry for her and criticizing the parents.

In parallel, the parents are moving from the status of "good losers" to "strong and bad winners." When their child doesn't observe the boundaries that have been set, they feel they are good but pathetic and helpless, whereas when boundaries are set and obeyed, they feel they are strong but guilty and bad. The stronger the child's reaction to the boundaries, the more guilty the parents feel.

If things keep going like that, the message to the child is that restrictive parenting is "bad" while "good" parenting is being permissive and never causing the child frustration.

Later in life, the child might regard other figures of authority, such as teachers, community leaders, commanding officers in the army, and bosses in a similar way. He might confront them and develop grudges and hostile feelings toward them.

The child might be very unlikely to accept any kind of authority, including that of the law, and he might also find it hard to be authoritative himself, for fear of seeing himself as "bad."

But, of course, judging people from the perspective of "strong" being "bad" and "weak" being "good" is in itself childish. A strong person can also be good and, as a matter of fact, a strong, winning parent is what a child needs most. Isn't this a combination that we all strive for? Don't we all want the "good guys" to win?

We believe that a child internalizes the combination of "strong" and "good" when he has boundaries set for him during his early years. With all the difficulties involved in setting boundaries, it is important to understand that the painful friction between parents and their children will, in time, gradually dissipate, as will the anger and resentment they arouse. Parents are gradually seen as "good guys" and the end of the process constitutes the internalization that the parental image is both strong and good.

When children grow up with the sense that their father is strong and good, they will build for themselves a positive self-image and will be quite sure that they, too, will be strong and good, like their dad. They will no longer need to control their environment in order to feel powerful. This kind of power is false. It carries with it feelings of guilt and social isolation, whereas real power is developed and nourished by positive behavior and constructive activity, which in turn provides a child with a sense of self-worth, satisfaction, and meaning.

> Noam had learning difficulties and high levels of energy. For him, the transition from his easy-going kindergarten to the demanding first grade classroom was difficult and frustrating. This frustration, combined with his anxiety and distress, sparked intense anger; he became rowdy and he cursed, ran wild, was violent toward his classmates, and destroyed property. During the day he was the terror of the school, and at night he was plagued by nightmares and unable to fall asleep.
>
> Psychologists, school counselors, and mentors all joined forces to help him. They proposed acceptance, understanding, and capitulation; to talk things through with him; and not to pressure or frustrate him. But things went from bad to worse and the road to a special school and social isolation seemed alarmingly short.
>
> In desperation, Noam's parents turned to a different kind of counseling, and this time the therapy offered a completely different approach. There would be no more unconditional acceptance; there would be no more talks and explanations, beseeching, or lecturing; no longer

would constant reaction and attention be the reward for unacceptable behavior. The therapist explained to the parents that from now on, **they** would be the ones to determine the agenda in their home. She instructed them to frustrate Noam in small, regular sessions, and taught them appropriate ways to respond to his behavior; negative but nondestructive behavior was to be completely ignored, whereas violent and hurtful behavior was to receive firm punishment, such as privileges being revoked for a lengthy period. The therapist explained to the parents that Noam's oddity aroused in them mixed feelings of anger, hate, and pity, which resulted in a need to compensate him and to smooth over any frustration on his behalf. The therapist explained to them that their enormous efforts to appease Noam, the endless attention, and the gifts they were constantly plying him with perpetuated his wretchedness, and that in order to strengthen him, it was important to frustrate him frequently, to connect him to his own pain, and to introduce him to real-life hardships with regard to his schoolwork and his social interactions. In order to achieve this, the therapist instructed the local educational team to conduct a comprehensive didactic analysis for Noam and she also recommended testing his motor abilities so they could be dealt with in a targeted manner. Noam was now obliged to deal with feelings he had previously escaped from—frustration, weakness, failure, and jealousy.

The many professionals who had previously been involved in Noam's treatment predicted that Noam's condition would deteriorate, but his condition only improved. His aggression and anxiety decreased significantly and were replaced by achievements in school and a reinforced social standing.

The test came in the course of a regional competition organized by the horse-riding group Noam belonged to. Knowing how scared Noam was of losing, his parents were tense and alert. To the surprise of everyone involved, Noam overcame his fears, mustered all his courage, mounted the horse, charged forward with the other competitors—and won!

While the large crowd was still applauding enthusiastically, it transpired that Noam was registered for an additional race. He was paralyzed with fear and announced that he wouldn't participate. His parents refused to allow him to withdraw from the race and Noam managed to overcome his fears and once again mounted the horse. This time he lost the race. Everyone expected a stormy reaction, tears, and anger, but no! Noam shed a few tears, recovered, and smiled. "You were right to force me to take part. I think it was important," he said.

Bogus strength and control gained by means of terror, threats, and violence had become a thing of the past. They were replaced by genuine strength. Noam learned how to cope with the pain of failure and contain it.

Chapter Eighteen

Morality and Assertiveness

Is a child who has been subjected to boundaries able to become assertive and stand up for his rights? Isn't there a danger of him becoming weak and submissive?

When Assi was three years old, his behavior became wild and aggressive. Every day when he returned from nursery school, he would make a mess of the house, beat his siblings, and destroy things. His parents did not give in to him. They used to punish him whenever it was necessary—once, twice, even ten times a day. Was he damaged?

Assi is now nine years old, a sociable boy with a pleasant disposition. He is a good student and loves to play football and read books. Assi respects his parents and still knows how to stand up for himself and does not hesitate to voice his opinions. One day, when his mother reprimanded him for his worrying habit of lingering on the way to and from school, he responded, "Mom, if you are this worried, it's not my problem. I'm nine years old—I should be able to chat with my friends and come home late. This is how we socialize."

Do parents who use force to punish raise a moral child? Are children who have had boundaries imposed on them capable of, for instance, defending someone weaker than themselves? Is there a possibility of them turning into heartless and subservient robots?

> Eleven-year-old Omer's parents believe in boundaries. The father is authoritative and is backed by the mother. In their home, violence is forbidden, as is bullying. The children are required to display patience toward their younger siblings and to help their parents with the housework. They are punished if they hurt one another. Omer accepts his parents' authority, has no problems at school, and interacts well with his peers.
>
> One day Omer heard his mother expressing her opinion that Israeli soldiers shouldn't have been endangered in the Jenin refugee camp during Operation Defensive Shield. She thought it was wrong that the IDF had refrained from using tanks in order to save the lives of innocent civilians. Omer turned to his mother and said, "I think you are wrong. If there are innocent people there, including women and children, it is important to make every effort to avoid hurting them, even if they are our enemies and even if by doing so our own soldiers are endangered." Omer certainly has morals and values. How did he acquire them?

Morals are not learned in lectures, nor are they internalized by means of explanations and theories. It's not enough to talk and preach morals. The ability to recognize the existence of the other, to respect his rights, and to behave toward him in a moral manner is developed through enforcing boundaries. A child cannot adopt values of defending society's weaker members if he is allowed to beat other children and bully them.

Parents who refrain from enforcing boundaries and think explanations are enough transmit to their child a message that boundaries are not obligatory and that they can be ignored.

The parents of Re'i Horev, a teenage boy who murdered Asaf Steierman, an innocent young boy, testified that they loved their son very much, taught him values, and stressed the importance of being considerate of one's peers. They undoubtedly really meant what they said. However, bitter reality proved that the fact that they loved their son and talked to him about morals had not prevented him from turning into a coldblooded murderer. Love is not enough!

Re'i Horev's ex-wife was interviewed for an important Israeli paper in November 2001 and said that she had wondered for a long time what had led Horev to such violence and cruelty.

Any reasonable and intelligent person would understand that a child doesn't simply turn into a monster. There must surely have been something in his childhood. Surely his parents are to blame. Perhaps [it was] a childhood trauma that had been repressed? Today I know that this isn't the case. He was raised in an atmosphere that provided no boundaries. Everything was allowed him. He always charmed everybody and he was always forgiven for everything he did. His anger against them [his parents] was irrational, for the very fact that they existed as his parents. He couldn't tolerate authority.

How can we restrict our children when we love them so much? When they are our own flesh and blood and the light of our lives?

The book of Proverbs gives us the answer: "For whom the LORD loveth He correcteth, even as a father the son in whom he delighteth" (3:12).

Chapter Nineteen

When There Is No Self-Control

Education and restraint—what is allowed and what is forbidden—are not only a social imperative, but also the emotional imperative of the individual, because they constitute the walls of one's "emotional" home and provide one with a sense of control, order, and organization. A world that has cyclicality, routine, laws, boundaries, and an environment that provides certainty, moderates the anxiety inherent in human existence. Adults are drawn to a world of routine and certainty, not to mention children, for whom every case of disrupted routine, however minor, can arouse anxiety. When routine is disrupted, in cases such as a visit to the doctor's office, or moving to a new home, children who have had boundaries set for them will cope relatively easily, whereas children who have not experienced boundaries will react to such events with anxiety. In an attempt to escape anxiety, they will riot and lash out in all directions, and they will not be calmed with a soft voice, lengthy explanations, and far-reaching promises.

When there is an even graver disruption to a child's routine, when events are exceptionally harsh and shocking and seriously upset the familiar pattern of a child's life, such as war, deportation, divorce, or the loss of a significant person, the level of helplessness increases, and with it, loss of control. The child becomes increasingly anxious and his world collapses. Under such extreme circumstances, parental authority and boundaries are essential in maintaining an atmosphere of "business as usual" to modify the uncertainties and anxieties that the child is experiencing.

In the absence of a strong parental presence, a child searches desperately for a sense of control and will try to obtain it at all costs, sometimes by taking control of the environment and sometimes through exaggerated and inappropriate self-control. A child is liable to develop a codex of laws all her own, which includes a series of strict and unrealistic prohibitions such as "I shouldn't eat," or, "I shouldn't let myself get fat," or, "I shouldn't speak," or, "I shouldn't get dirty," and this can quickly turn into a serious obsessive compulsive disorder. We believe that such an emotional-behavioral disturbance, which appears to have a firm biological basis, also relies on a lack of boundaries and a child's desperate attempts to achieve self-control in response to the anxiety to which she is prone (19-1).

When parents, teachers, and therapists observe a child who willingly adopts a system of harsh rules and extreme demands, they tend to think that the child is being cruel to himself and, since the general opinion is that this is an internalization of overly harsh parental images (19-2), therapy directs the parents to embrace their child with warmth and love, to soften attitudes toward him, and to pity him. However, as much as the child needs to be loved, this love should be expressed in a different way.

Ronit is the third daughter in a well-heeled family with six children. Her father, David, a wealthy businessman, has spoiled his children and provided them with everything they could possibly want. Their mother, Rachel, a schoolteacher, gave up her job when she started having children and devoted all her time and energy to raising them. Ronit received boundless love and attention and enjoyed all the material pleasures that money can buy. She was an introverted and shy girl but was fond of the good things in life, especially the food that her mother was so good at cooking.

The family tended toward overachievement and the girls aspired to excel in everything. Ronit also aspired to excel and applied enormous effort to her schoolwork. Her mother would often find her in the morning asleep at her desk. The education system noted her pleasing achievements, but did not discern Ronit's problems in school, which intensified as her curriculum became increasingly complex. Her constant ambition to excel and to be like her sisters extracted a high price from Ronit, who, by the end of sixth grade, when she was twelve years old, began to fail. She felt that she was overweight and started to starve herself. She became anorexic.

At first, her mother did not notice what was happening to her daughter. Since all her children were thin, she did not notice that Ronit was especially so. When matters deteriorated and Ronit's skin turned gray, her mother feared that the girl had cancer. She had no idea that this was a case of anorexia. In the small village where the family lived, they had never even heard of the disorder. One day Ronit collapsed and her parents took her to the emergency room at the local hospital. At a height of 160 cm, Ronit weighed just twenty-seven kilos. Her parents were told that their daughter was suffering from anorexia and had to be hospitalized in a psychiatric hospital. They found it hard to accept the news and refused to allow their daughter to be admitted to a mental health facility.

Life in the previously happy and ebullient family home became unbearable. The other children witnessed quarrels and endless raised voices, tears, and anger. Ronit's condition continued to deteriorate until she reached a weight of twenty-two kilos.

She was then hospitalized in an inpatient unit for eating disorders. She was fed intravenously until her weight increased, after many months, to fifty-five kilos. Along with her weight gain, Ronit underwent an additional process—her fellow patients at the facility taught her several highly sophisticated maneuvers for fooling the medical team. She learned how to lie and conceal food; she destroyed computers, telephones, and doors; she learned how to carry out suicide attempts. As usual, she did everything perfectly and soon turned into the most difficult patient on the ward.

Ronit had a rule book all her own. She was allowed to cheat, curse, destroy, and scream, but she was not allowed to eat or get dirty. She restricted her spheres of interest and built herself a new and corrupted agenda in which there was only room for compulsive activity, rituals, and self-starvation.

One by one the doctors gave up, and came to the tragic conclusion that Ronit would probably never be rehabilitated and would never be able to live beyond the confines of a mental health facility.

Her parents asked the doctors to give Ronit one more chance to live at home and they agreed, on the condition that her father, David, keep her under round-the-clock observation. David gave up his job and stayed close to the family home. The family was weakened in every possible way. Ronit's mother fell into depression; her father lost his entire fortune and sank into heavy debt. It seemed like there was no way out.

As the family's weakness increased, Ronit's condition deteriorated. Her body became emaciated, depleted, distorted, and bent. Her hands were covered in sores from having been washed obsessively hundreds of times a day. By this time there was no alternative but to hospitalize her again in a mental health facility. The doctors diagnosed her as an incurable mental patient and advised her father to come to terms with the fact that he had lost one of his daughters.

As Passover approached, David asked to take his daughter home for a vacation so that she could attend the family Seder. Although the doctors feared she might harm herself, they agreed to let her out for a brief furlough.

On the way home, Ronit tried to jump out of the car window and her father was forced to hold on to her as he drove. However, to everyone's surprise, during the holiday meal she sat and ate with great gusto. No one present had the slightest inkling of Ronit's secret plan. She had decided to enjoy one last meal before finally putting an end to her life. She was unable to continue to fast and she didn't want to return to the psychiatric hospital. After the meal, she sneaked to her room and swallowed dozens of pills she had been hoarding over the months she'd spent at the hospital. She swallowed them one by one and waited to die. But, with the same impulsiveness that had driven her to swallow the pills, Ronit decided to choose life. She crawled to the door and called out to her parents.

Late that night, her father's car sped to the local hospital and the unconscious Ronit was admitted to the intensive care unit. It was there that the family met for the first time with the doctor who saved the girl's life. After Ronit regained consciousness, the doctor asked to speak to her mother. The girl was sprawled across the bed, her body distorted, and she was screaming and cursing indiscriminately.

Her mother stayed with her and refused to leave her. No amount of pleas or beseeching would help and it was necessary to use force to separate mother from daughter, who continued to scream for a few minutes longer before falling silent.

For hours on end Rachel told her daughter's painful story, at the end of which the doctor explained the main points of her own therapeutic approach. The doctor talked about Ronit's intense anxiety. She stressed the importance of parental strength and authority, the essential need for setting clear boundaries, and the necessity for the emotional separation of the girl from her mother as a means to ease the anxiety. It all sounded very distant, strange, and foreign. The doctor spoke about a "firm hand," about the denial of attention and privileges. Rachel reacted with shock. She had never been spoken to in this way. The doctors she encountered in the past spoke of a grave illness, they spoke of medication, they talked about a grim future. No one had ever talked to her about discipline, about a "firm hand," about sanctions. No one had ever before related to Ronit as a child with learning difficulties rather than a seriously sick girl. The previous therapists had never made a connection between the lack of parental boundaries and authority and the emotional disturbances their daughter had developed.

At the end of the lengthy session, Rachel said that she might possibly be able to implement the doctor's therapeutic approach, but she stressed that David, being utterly controlled by his daughter,would never be able to face up to her and put an end to her demands. The doctor wouldn't back down and that very afternoon, she summoned David to her office.

David listened to what the doctor had to say, understood the logic in it, and immediately connected with it. He offered his full cooperation.

As soon as Ronit came out of the ICU, she was sent back to the mental health facility where she had been hospitalized before. However, after no change was observed in her condition, her father removed her from the facility against the advice of her therapists and placed her in the sole care of the new doctor, who by that time he looked up to as his daughter's savior.

The main points of her subsequent therapy, in Ronit's words:

I was summoned to the therapy center. The doctor sat opposite me and ordered me to write a sentence on a sheet of paper. I sat in front of her, bent over and refused adamantly. She ordered me to sit up straight, but I didn't want to. She stood up and walked over to me, and then she tried to force my shoulders straight. I became angry and jumped at her, cursing her and shouting, "Who do you think you are?" The doctor was unfazed. She forced my shoulders to straighten. I looked at my father who didn't say a word and cried from the shock of it.

Another time, the doctor gave me rice and noodles to eat. I didn't like it and threw the plate down on the floor. She jumped toward me and ordered me to clean it all up. Again, I was in shock.

The doctor then realized that I was obsessive about cleanliness and terribly frightened of dirt. The counselors had told her that I refuse to get dirty and won't even touch gouache paint. She came up to me and smeared my hands with paint. I went berserk, crying and swearing. "You're going to learn to get yourself dirty," she said. I thought she'd ruined my life, that it was her fault that I was now ugly and filthy and I soaped my hands at least ten times. But in spite of the shock, I learned to dirty myself with paints (Yehudit Yehezkeli, *Yedioth Aharonot*, April 25, 2000).

The therapy process lasted about a year and was riddled with crises and regressions. Ronit's parents were given extensive guidance in setting boundaries and after a three-year absence Ronit returned to school. She received a great deal of help and corrective education, did well in school, and managed to bridge the gaps she had accumulated. Her confidence in her ability to cope with the demands of the school system gradually grew and she succeeded in her matriculation exams and became socially accepted by her classmates. After graduating from high school, she found employment, got married, and gave birth to her first daughter.

What secret lies behind this success? What was the reason for the failure of the accepted empathetic approach?

We believe that success sprang from a profound understanding of the emotional processes that Ronit went through.

> Anorexia allowed Ronit to escape reality. It enabled her to ignore the demands of her teachers, to escape the anxieties of puberty, the necessity to integrate into her peer group, and her feelings of dependency and weakness. Every time she conquered her desire to eat, she felt strong, and every ounce she managed to shed contributed to her sense of power. She celebrated every victory over her parents and immediate vicinity. Her false sense of power grew stronger and blurred her feelings of anxiety and helplessness. As her illness grew worse, Ronit's secondary gains increased, because she won love, attention, and the endless consideration of her family. For a while it was enough for Ronit, but soon she decompensated and her anxiety mounted. The more anxious she was, the more her self-confidence deteriorated and the greater her need for control became.
>
> Her therapy did not attempt to cancel out Ronit's need for control, but rather to block it, like a dam stopping a huge flow of water and redirecting it toward more desirable channels like studying, painting, socializing, and so on. Ronit's false sense of power was taken away from her and while her parents resumed their authority and no longer gave in to her unhealthy demands, she was now able to trust them and view them as strong and reliable. She could now lean on them and feel secure and relax, and could benefit from the professional help she was offered. From that point on, the road to recovery was assured.

Chapter Twenty

When Authority Is Absent

"The boy lashes out and swears? It must be because of the way he was treated as a child."

"The girl behaves violently. It must be because her parents weren't sufficiently attentive...she must have felt unloved..."

"An abused child will grow up to become an abusive parent" (20-1).

"The child is running wild? He should be allowed to get it out of his system. It's not good for him to suppress his feelings. It might all come bursting out when he's older."

We tend to relate to this nonsense as if it came straight from the mouth of God, even when cold reality hits us daily in the face.

Enlightened countries like Austria and Scandinavia, where laws against corporal punishment have been passed, have now risen to the top of the list of western countries with the highest rates of juvenile violence. "The Scandinavians are shocked to discover that they are among the leaders in the crime list," reported *Yedioth Aharonot* in November 2003, while according to *Ha'aretz* (November 5, 2003), Israel has seen a 54 percent increase in violence of schoolchildren against their teachers.

We are not surprised. As we see it, the damage done to parental authority as well as to teachers' authority, whether through legislation or as a result of public pressure, is the ultimate direct cause of the increase in children's lack of inhibition and increased levels of violence. When authority is threatened, restricted, and weakened, and when children know that it is acceptable to call the police whenever parents or teachers punish them, violence will break out and take control of everything. In his book *Power and Compassion*, family therapist Jerome Price warns of the danger that awaits families as the result of exaggerated infringement on their autonomy and authority by law-enforcement authorities. Foundations have been established in the United States in support of parents' rights, such as Parents for Children (*The Detroit News*, February 6, 2002), that warn against delegitimizing educational authorities. This grim picture of the situation shows that even though prosecuting parents does indeed prevent a few cases of child abuse, it is still the cause of the destruction of many families. Indeed, with the rise of public initiatives to limit parental authority, we are witnessing a dramatic rise in juvenile violence (examples and statistics can be found in the media).

Decades ago, sociologist Philip Rieffe (20-2) foresaw the problematic results of what he referred to as "the triumph of the psychotherapy." Rieffe pointed to the potential paradox that is created when educational authorities deny the right of people in authoritative positions to carry out their authority to educate. In the book, *A Dispirited Rebellion* by Gadi Taub, there are quite a few illustrations of this situation in Israel (20-3).

Paterson, a well-known researcher in the field of child and adolescent behavioral disorders, did an about-turn in his position when he was confronted by reality. In the early days of his career, Paterson was convinced that educators should be lenient with children and that only positive reinforcements should be used. After many years of research, he came to the complete opposite conclusion—only punishment could curtail antisocial behavior (20-4).

Dunham et al. underwent a similar process. When they studied the effect of counseling for parents coping with their children's behavioral problems, they found that, contrary to their basic assumption, demonstrating positive feelings toward nursery-age children without setting boundaries did not lead to any improvement in the children's problematic behavior. Improvement was observed only among children whose parents set clear boundaries and gave clear directions (20-5).

Paterson concludes from his studies that the emergence of an aggressive child occurs when a temperamental child meets inconsistent parents. He also concludes that a high-strung child needs to have boundaries set for him before he reaches one year of age. According to Paterson, a two-year-old who suffers from temper tantrums with no significant response from his parents will grow up to be a violent bully, will find it hard to deal with the demands of frameworks, and, in adulthood, will likely turn to a life of crime.

According to Paterson, violence is genetic and is not a sign of trauma or of repressed problems. He is therefore convinced that for the good of the child and of his environment, violence should be curbed and its expression restricted. This approach, which echoes Freud's later teachings (20-6), conforms to the major psychological concepts that deal with the sources of human aggression.

Another concept has it that aggression is not inherent but is the result of parental aggression toward the child, so that a child who has experienced violence will grow up to be a violent adult (20-7). In the spirit of this concept, therapists preach to parents that they must approach their child with understanding and forgiveness and not anger, because a child "who experienced anger from his environment will become angry, and a child who has grown up being criticized will tend to criticize." This approach is also accepted in Israel and its slogans are splashed across the walls of local kindergartens and schools.

We share the idea that aggression is a genetic urge and in the absence of authority to dole out punishment, demand respect, and restrain the child, sooner or later this aggression will emerge.

From literature, as well as from our own experience, we have learned that children who are afflicted with motor skills disorders, as well as learning or social difficulties, are exceptionally sensitive to the absence of authority, boundaries, and frameworks, and there is a real danger of such children growing up to be aggressive and violent, or fearful and sad.

The logic is simple. Children who suffer from any kind of disorder experience higher levels of frustration, weakness, failure, disappointment, anger, and anxiety. They also develop low self-esteem, and in an attempt to obtain a consolatory sense of control and power, they develop psychopathology. The stronger ones develop aggression and violence that provide them with control over their parents and their environment, whereas the weaker ones turn against themselves and develop somatic symptoms or other symptoms of anxiety that also have the potential to exert control over their family and their environment, albeit in a passive form. A child who develops aggressive behavior has to cope with social rejection, or with being removed from frameworks, and eventually becomes a danger to himself and to society. On the other hand, a child who develops overt anxiety symptoms might develop a lifelong mental illness. Boundaries and authoritative figures can ameliorate such dangerous situations because they make it possible to approach the child, treat his disabilities, and improve his self-esteem.

> Nine-year-old Matan is an only child. His mother believes in a permissive educational approach, whereas his father, although he believes differently, gives in to his wife's uncompromising position. At the age of two, Matan was diagnosed as a violent child, and as soon as he entered school he started beating other children as well as adults, and he destroyed everything within his reach. Because of his violent behavior, he has been expelled from his previous school and placed in a small class. He has subsequently been expelled from this class as well, and finally placed in a special school for children with behavioral disorders.
>
> Due to his serious behavioral problems, Matan underwent several therapeutic attempts typical of the empathic approach, all of which were to no avail. His condition deteriorated and his concerned and exhausted parents finally found a psychiatrist who believed in a different approach. During their first meeting, Matan stormed into

the room and immediately set about turning it upside down. The doctor ordered him to rearrange the room immediately; Matan responded, "Ask me nicely and I'll decide if I feel like cleaning it up."

To his parents this behavior was "an assertive reaction on behalf of the boy" and they supported him.

The doctor thought differently and, with a stern expression on her face, she told Matan that he would not be leaving the room until he cleaned it up. "What?" shouted Matan. "You think you can tell me what to do? You think you can speak to me like that?!" And he promptly launched into an attack on the doctor, furiously hitting and kicking her. His parents were horrified, but didn't raise a finger. The doctor ordered the father to hold Matan until he calmed down. Matan screamed, threatened to call the police, kicked, and cursed. But he calmed down slowly and his father let go of him. The doctor repeated her order to clean up the room, and this time the boy cooperated willingly.

The doctor diagnosed Matan as suffering from extremely high levels of anxiety as well as learning difficulties that had previously gone undetected. She explained to the boy's parents that their son had wrapped himself in a heavy armor of violence and never allowed anyone to approach him to touch his real pain; the educational system had never been wise enough to identify and address his difficulties.

His mother found it hard to watch the restraints imposed on Matan and was able to relax only when she was convinced that no damage had been done to him. Matan, on the other hand, did not appear in the least upset. On the contrary, his face lit up and actually glowed; he smiled in all directions and seemed happy, as if in relief. His anxiety decreased and he was able to behave normally.

The doctor encouraged Matan's parents to take on their son's treatment, fully aware that what they had all just experienced together would help them to better cope with his difficulties. From now on they would not stand helplessly in front of their son's aggression. Things were different now. They understood that Matan's learning disabilities and his highly volatile nature had been exposing him to situations of anxiety and perpetuating his already low self-esteem. They understood that the important thing now was to set clear boundaries for Matan in order to boost his sense of security and to provide him with the ability to channel his energies in ways that would lead him to success. By understanding the principles of the proposed therapy, Matan's parents were able to internalize them and implement them at home.

Matan was a success story! But he is not the only child whose aggression puts him at a disadvantage.

An aggressive and violent child is a lonely child. He is prone to be rejected by his peers and, in more extreme situations, even expelled from normative educational frameworks. He might suffer from isolation because he arouses feelings of anger and revulsion among those who are most important in his life—**even his own parents.**

Chapter Twenty-One

Parental Love

In her article "Our Adult World and Its Roots in Infancy," Melanie Klein warns, "Parents who do not restrict their child are liable to feel some resentment toward him that will seep into their relationship and pollute it" (257).

In a similar vein, Paterson's article, published in 1982, that deals with the connection between child aggression and maternal rejection, raises the question of the chicken and the egg (21-1). Patterson asks whether it is rejection on the part of the mother that arouses the child's aggression, or whether the child's unruly behavior is what causes the mother's rejection. From the research, it appears that the child's aggressive and demanding behavior arouses in his mother feelings of rejection toward him and not the other way round. Further, exaggerated parental leniency and the desire to indulge their child and maintain a good relationship with him serve to encourage his aggression, which in turn arouses the parents' rejection and results in the child losing much of the emotional closeness and intimacy he needs with his parents.

Five-year-old Rami is an only child. His parents are divorced and he lives with his mother. Because of her liberal worldview, the mother refrains from imposing boundaries on her son, whereas the father, who sees his son twice a week, pampers him and "buys" him with gifts. Rami goes to a special needs kindergarten and, since his responses to any restriction or refusal are unruly, the teacher is not interested in confrontations with him and permits him to do whatever he wants. At home, too, every "no" causes him to run wild. He attacks his mother, kicks and hits her, breaks and destroys glass objects, decorative knick-knacks, and electronics.

When Rami is in the throes of an anger attack, his parents look on helplessly. His father admits painfully that his son's behavior is so troubling as to sometimes cause him to feel that children are not a joyful blessing.

How sad!

How does it happen that parents who are so full of good intentions reach a point where they are disgusted by their own children?

How does it happen that parents become paralyzed in the presence of their small children?

Why do parents fear to scold, punish, and to make demands of their children, as if these would be tantamount to criminal behavior?

How has parenting been destroyed?

How does it come about that children and youths beat and kick each other, put each other in physical danger, cause physical harm to each other, and also to adults—and this is considered acceptable, normal behavior?

Itamar, father of Nimrod and Ilan, is a warmhearted, pleasant-natured man—a man who cares. He is a man who often places himself at the disposal of others and tries to be a model father. He invests a lot in his children and treats them with warmth and gentleness. He doesn't understand, therefore, why his older son, Nimrod, a strong, thickset boy, makes a habit of cruelly beating his younger brother, Ilan, pulling his hair and smashing toys against him, completely unprovoked and for no reason. Itamar tried to stop Nimrod. He told him no and to stop it, but to no avail; Nimrod continued to abuse his brother and Itamar gave up and stopped scolding him. "I could see that it was bigger than him, so I let him do it," he said. The sight of a two-year-old child subjected to the bullying of his older brother was unpleasant. Hardest of all was the fact that Ilan did not even ask his father, who was standing nearby, for help. It was as if the little boy had already given up on the possibility that any kind of authority could protect him from his brother's aggression.

A six-year-old child unleashes his aggressive urges and beats his small brother and their father stands by helplessly, watching the horrible display.

How can a father stand by helplessly in front of his six-year-old son, certain that he is not allowed to punish him, even when he knows that the punishment is meant to stop the boy's violence?

Does Itamar, like other parents, behave in such a way because he doesn't care about his younger son? Does he not love him?

Or have we all lost our sanity and been drawn along on the zeitgeist that has taken the issue of children's rights to a ridiculous extreme?

We seem to have forgotten that modern psychology developed at a time when parental authority was absolute and children were devoid of all rights. In modern western society, the situation is the complete opposite. Children have accumulated so much power that they have become corrupted by it, and we are witnessing a reality in which some children have become violent bullies and even murderers.

Chapter Twenty-Two

Reality, Not Hypocrisy

What, then, is our vision?

A generation of children all cut from the same cloth?

Of course not!

True, the human genome has been cracked, but human behavior is still an enigma. Children are still not available to order. There is no such thing as a perfect human being.

There will always be children who are over-competitive, over-possessive/materialistic, and over-anxious. This does not mean that we'll stop loving and educating our children.

Boundaries were not invented to create the perfect child, but rather to enable a child—with her inherent characteristics—to better integrate into various frameworks and to better cope with frustration and anxiety. A child who has internalized the boundaries set for her grows into an adult who is sensitive to others, empathetic to their pain, and able to maintain relationships that are based on equality and closeness.

By removing parents' natural and spontaneous responses and neutering their authority, a whole generation of children is growing up with little respect for their fellow beings and for themselves, and who make their lives and those of their families unbearable.

Unfortunately, in our society the setting of boundaries has lost its legitimacy. Parents are wicked—this is the message. They are to blame, they understand nothing, and justice is not on their side. Law and custom are constantly restricting parents' normal scope of response. So long as this situation continues, we shall keep seeing young people either resorting to violence and intimidation, or being anxious and frightened.

In an organized society, anyone who spurns the authority of parents and teachers might end up spurning legal authorities.

"Children can be raised without punishment, without being threatened with punishment, without fear"—what hypocrisy this is!!

Indeed there are children for whom no punishment is necessary and for whom only a slight change in the tone of one's voice is enough to bring them back on track. These are children who have an easy temperament. They are the nice children—other people's children.

Our children need boundaries. We are not talking here of a Victorian upbringing, or cold, cruel, Prussian parenting. There is no contradiction between warm and loving parenting and the setting of boundaries; indeed, it's quite the opposite.

The mother who cradles her little baby in her arms to lull him into sleep is the same mother who punishes him when he bites his brother or lashes out at his friends in kindergarten. The father who rocks his baby in his arms during long nights of earaches is the very same father who scolds and punishes his daughter when she curses or refuses to take a bath.

Should parents be flexible? Flexibility is the ability to respond differently to a child under different circumstances and at different ages; it's the ability to behave both gently and firmly and to respond differentially to a three-year-old and a ten-year-old (22-1).

Parental flexibility is the ability to wonder at a child's first drawing and to become tearfully emotional at the first words a child utters, and, on the other hand, to raise one's voice, to stop with a rebuke a child's attempt to stick his fingers into an electric socket, and to punish him when he kicks or bites his younger sibling or his friends.

We have been accustomed to perceive children as being a persecuted minority in need of protection from the cruelty of parents, and the result is that we have denied parents the ability to protect their own children.

Parents are not meant to be angels.

Parenting means loving a child, taking responsibility for her life and safety, feeding, dressing, encouraging, comforting, working on her behalf without reservations, and raising her to be a mature person. Parenting also means educating, restricting, stopping, and demanding. It is not a case of either or; it is a case of both.

End Notes

Chapter 1, note number 1:

Haley, J. (1986). *Uncommon Therapy: The Psychiatric Techniques of Milton H. Erikson, M.D.* (pp. 213–217). New York and London: W.W. Norton & Company. (First published 1973)

Chapter 1, note number 2:

Kernberg, O. (1984). *Severe Personality Disorders: Psychotherapeutic Strategies* (pp. 275–289). New Haven and London: Yale University Press.

In his book, Kernberg defines various levels of superego integration. According to his definition, integrative superego is what allows a child to feel appropriate guilt and moral responsibility for the other, as well as to behave in accordance with accepted moral codes.

Chapter 2, note number 1:

Ibid., p. 278. Kernberg relates to the difference between recognizing the accepted boundaries and morality, and moral behavior. He differentiates between people who behave according to boundaries, laws, and moral codes (in our language, people with integrative superego) and those who do not behave morally, hurt others, and regard law and morality as a mere suggestion. In other words, they are familiar with the law and the moral demands, but they do not behave accordingly. Kernberg defines them as "psychopaths."

Chapter 2, note number 2:

Haley, J. (1986). *Uncommon Therapy: The Psychiatric Techniques of Milton H. Erickson, M.D.* (p. 213). New York and London: W.W. Norton & Company.

Chapter 2, note number 3:

On the importance of the unanimous parental stand with regard to setting boundaries, see Prof. Yoel Goldberg's *Disciplinary problems among children*, 1987,pp. 53–54, Tel Aviv, Zmora Bitan Publishers.

Chapter 2, note number 4:

The assumption is that object integration is not assured, even when the frustration caused to the child/baby is not severe in a way that will lead him to turn to the mechanism of splitting.

An additional and essential condition for forming integration of the internal object is the presence of a parent, who is behaving as such—both good and frustrating, in accordance with the child's age. The assumption is that the process of forming the object image does not occur only in the first few months of the baby's life (when a parent's objective is to reduce his baby's frustration as much as possible), but during the first few years, while a parent, who sets boundaries, is the frustrating agent. The idea that creating an image of a whole object happens when the object is being frustrating is not new, and one can spot it in Edith Jacobson's theoretical thinking. (See S. Mitchell and M.J. Black's *Freud and Beyond: A History of Modern Psychoanalytic Thought*, published by Basic Books, Perseus Books Group, pp. 48–53).

Chapter 3, note number 1:

Freud, S. (1927). The future of an illusion. In James Strachey (Ed.), *The Standard Edition of the Complete Psychological Works of Sigmund Freud* (Vol. 21, pp. 5–56). London: Hogarth Press and the Institute of Psycho-Analysis.

Freud, S. (1930). Civilization and its discontents. Ibid. (Vol. 21, pp. 64–145).

Freud, S. (1933). New Introductory Lectures on Psychoanalysis, Lecture 34: Explanations, applications and orientations. Ibid. (Vol. 22, pp. 163–157).

Freud thought that aggression is inherent. According to him, most humans need to be in a social surrounding and are unable to live alone. If their aggression and impulses are not restricted by education, society will not be able to exist.

Chapter 3, note number 2:

Baumrind, D. (1973). *The Development of Instrumental Competence through Socialization* (Vol. 7, pp. 3–45). Minnesota Symposium on Child Psychology.

Chapter 3, note number 3:

Woodward, L.J., Fergusson, D.M., & Horwood, L.J. (2002). Romantic relationships of young people with childhood and adolescent onset antisocial behavior problems. *Journal of Abnormal Child Psychology, 3*(30), 231–243.

Kokko, K., & Pulkikinen, L. (2000). Aggression in childhood and long-term unemployment in adulthood: A cycle of Maladaptation and some protective factors. *Developmental Psychology, 36*(4), 463–472.

Moffitt, T.E., Caspi, A., Harrington, H., & Milne, B.J. (2002). Males on the life-course-persistent and adolescence–limited antisocial pathways: Follow-up at age 26 years. *DevelopmentalPsychopathology, 14*, 179–207.

Chapter 3, note number 4:

Spitz, R.A. (1957). *No and Yes: On the Genesis of Human Communication*. New York: International Universities Press.

In the 1950s, the psychoanalyst René Spitz published his book *No and Yes*, in which he claims that a child's ability to say no is built upon the "no" that he himself hears from his parents, and the frustration that this "no" arouses is one of the building blocks of the superego. After a child has heard "no" from his parents at some time between the ages of nine months to fifteen months, he begins to use the word "no" when he interacts with them.

We believe that one of the reasons that certain people find it hard to set boundaries is because they had no experience of having had boundaries set for them by their own parents. An adult who does not have childhood experiences of boundaries being set for him by his parents will find it hard to see them as a legitimate and integral part of a relationship. He will try to avoid having to set boundaries until he can no longer do so and then he'll explode, or break off the relationship. This explosion and/or break-off of the relationship are the result of the difficulty in setting boundaries. He will also find it hard to have boundaries set for him and will tend to break off the relationship in such situations.

Chapter 3, note number 5:

Masterson has a similar approach.

Masterson, J.F. (1985). *Treatment of the Borderline Adolescent: A Developmental Approach* (p. 106). New York: Bunner/Magel, Inc. (First published by Wiley Interscience, New York, 1972)

Chapter 3, note number 6:

Leowald, H.W. (1962). Internalization, Separation, Mourning and the Superego. *Psychoanalytic Quarterly, 31*, 483–504.

The psychoanalyst Leowald states that in the course of his development, a child internalizes the conflicts with his parents who limit, make demands, and expect. This is how superego and emotions are formed. Parents' responses to disruptive behavior in their child serve—once they are internalized—as internal warning signs against making wrong choices; parents' approval, demands, and expectations serve—once they are internalized—as a permanent source of motivation and pride when achieving and making ethical decisions. Paraphrasing Leowald, the superego is a representative of the future inner self (ibid., p. 501).

Chapter 3, note number 7:

Taub, G. (1997). *A Dispirited Rebellion*(pp. 68–84). Tel Aviv: Hakibbutz Hameuhad Publishers. (Hebrew)

Chapter 4, note number 1:

Masterson, J.F. (1985). *Treatment of the Borderline Adolescent: A Developmental Approach.* New York: Brunner/Mazel, Inc. (First published by Wiley Interscience, New York, 1972)

Masterson's book deals at length with boundaries and their effects on parent-child relations. When parents refrain from setting boundaries for their child, and let him do whatever he wants, the child feels that his parents are afraid of him. Masterson quotes one of his patients who said, "My parents never spanked me on my bottom—maybe they cared for me, but they were afraid of me" (p. 126). According to Masterson, as a result of this type of relationship his patient tended to treat his parents with disdain on one hand, and, on the other hand, expected the environment to treat him in a lenient way (p. 127). Both situations are undesirable.

Worse still, refraining from setting boundaries is perceived by the child not only as a sign of parental weakness, but also as neglect (p. 114).

Boundaries and the struggles over them are also a test for the parents' competence, trustworthiness, and reliability (pp. 110, 114).

According to Masterson, setting boundaries is essential for a child, since it helps him to cope with the anarchy of his impulses (p. 106). By having boundaries set for him, a child gradually learns self-control, which serves as the basis of his self-esteem, independence, and autonomy, and releases him from the control of his impulses (pp. 107,108).Without boundaries, a child is entirely enslaved by his hedonic needs (ibid.). He yearns for his parents' control, and when they loosen it, he feels left alone (p. 49).

In addition, boundaries at home allow a child to come to terms with school frameworks and get satisfaction from his academic and social achievements, instead of living in fantasy (p. 106).

Curbing a child's aggression helps him develop and maintain social skills, which will subsequently enable him to enjoy popularity among his peers (p. 115).

Supporters of Masterson's teachings are familiar with his claims that permissive parental attitudes are a response to the guilt parents feel for having abandoned their child too early.

We believe that today's over-permissive approach, which is more widespread than ever, is not only the result of parental guilt for rejecting or abandoning a child, but also a reflection of the zeitgeist.

Masterson attributes the sad state of the youths he treated both to neglect and the conciliatory attitudes they encountered during their childhood. A close study of the case histories in Masterson's book gives the impression that the struggles of the patients with their therapist over boundaries unleashed enormous amounts of emotion. When he interpreted their miserable state as a result of parental indulgence, he created an immediate bond with his patients, whereas an interpretation of parental estrangement aroused lukewarm responses. According to Masterson, this was a result of defensiveness. We assume that it testifies to the centrality of boundary-setting in developing the parent-child relationship.

Chapter 5, note number 1:

Freud, S. (1927). The Future of an Illusion. *SE,* Vol. *21*, 5–56, 40.

Freud, A. (1936). Chapter 5. *The Ego and the Mechanisms of Defense*. London: Hogarth Press and the Institute of Psycho-Analysis.

Winnicott, D.W. (1972). Fragments of an Analysis (p. 524). In: P.L. Giovacchini (Ed.), *Tactics and Techniques in Psychoanalytic Therapy.* M.D.Science House, Inc.

Jacobson, E., M.D. (1965). *The Self and the Object World* (pp. 122–124). London: Hogarth Press and the Institute of Psycho-Analysis.

Chapter 6, note number 1:

Baum, C.G., & Forehand, R. (1981). Long-term follow-up and assessment of parent training by use of multiple outcome measures. *Behavior Therapy, 12*, 643–652.

The abovementioned research deals with the effects of a parents' guidance program on their children's behavior. It discusses children aged between four and twelve who were verbally and physically aggressive. The parents were instructed to respond as follows: If the child was being aggressive, the parent was to punish him by using "time-out" (sitting in a chair for a few minutes), and if the child ignored this order he had to be punished again. On the other hand, the parents were instructed to provide the child with positive reinforcements for obedient and coordinated behavior. The results of the study testify to the success of the program. Follow-ups were conducted between one and four-and-a-half years after the parents were given instructions.

Howard, B.J. (1996). Advising parents on discipline: What works. *Pediatrics, 98*(4), 809–815.

In this paper, Howard provides guidelines for parents on the subject of discipline. She defines "education" as increasing appropriate behaviors and curbing inappropriate behaviors. The objective of the education, in her opinion, is to bring a child into being competent and able to guide and control himself.

A child's temperament, according to Howard, is an extremely significant element in his education. According to her, children with stormy temperaments are "hard" to educate.

In her studies, positive reinforcement and refraining from punishing these children offered no solution, and neither did verbal criticism or rejection. These measures, according to her, result in a rise in undesirable behaviors.

Ignoring the behaviors helped with only a few of the children and only when it came as a response to lack of attentiveness.

The most useful disciplinarian response, according to Howard, was "time-out." It meant sitting the child in a chair for a few minutes, or confining a child in his room or in the bathroom. Howard points out that "time-out" has to last several minutes with the parents remaining consistent. If a child runs away from the "time-out" room, Howard recommends giving him a spank on the behind, or shutting him in a room for a few minutes.

When parents issued a warning and threatened punishment, there was no change in behavior. Aggressive children even exacerbated their aggressive behavior in response to this particular approach.

Howard found that taking a toy away from a child is effective as a punishment. For children aged over twelve years, she recommends confinement.

Consistent punishment has a positive effect on child-parent relations, since when a child's behavior improves, his parents also undergo a positive change in attitude toward him. They listen to him more and order him around less.

Larzelere, R.E. (1998). Combining love and limits in disciplinary responses. Paper presented at the Conference on Parenthood in America, Madison, WI.

Larzelere reports on results of various studies, including those he himself conducted. One of the studies, for example, examines the effect of punishing as compared to the effect of explaining on aggressive behavior and lack of discipline among two- and three-year-old children. He found that combining punishment and explanation is more effective than the use of each tactic alone. The difference is mainly noticed in the sphere of physical aggressiveness, where the abovementioned combination leads to a very marked reduction in a child's aggressive behavior. Moreover, it was found that the behavior of children who were punished deteriorated only infrequently. The follow-up continued for twenty months.

Larzelere also relates to the results of Roberts's studies and suggests a model of imposing parental discipline in stages. The first stage consists of giving both an order and an explanation. If their child does not cooperate, the parents move on to a light punishment (like sitting in a chair). When the child continues to be uncooperative, the parents move on to an educational spank on the behind, or confining the child to his room.

Larzelere claims that his model conforms to previous research findings that indicate that there is a significant difference between disciplining "easy" children and disciplining children with stormy temperaments. While the parent of an "easy" child can suffice with demanding and explaining, the parent of a "difficult" child needs to use more severe measures, such as punishing him.

Chapter 6, note number 2:

Study 1:

Bean, A.W., & Roberts, M.W. (1981). The effect of time-out release contingencies on changes in child noncompliance. *Journal of Abnormal Child Psychology, 9,* 95–105.

The study examines the effect of parents' guidance approach on aggressive behavior (tantrums, beating, etc.) among two- to six-year-old children.

The children were divided into three groups:

In the first group, the mother was instructed to use a "time-out" (two minutes of sitting in a chair in the corner of the room) in response to the child's aggressive behavior (including tantrums). The mother was told that if the child got up before he was allowed, she should give him a spanking on the behind and force him back into the chair.

Children in this group received an average of eight spankings until they cooperated with the "time-out" demand. None of them cooperated with the two-minute "time-out" without at least one spanking.

In the second group, the child was given a "time-out" and permission to decide for himself when to get out of the chair.

In the third group, the children were not punished at all for their behavior.

Results show that children in the first group, in which parents had absolute control, improved their behavior to the extent that they stopped having behavioral problems altogether. In the second group, children's behavior improved temporarily, but they continued to have some behavioral problems. In the third group, children showed no improvement whatsoever in their behavior.

Study 2:

Day,D.E, &Roberts, M.W. (1983). An Analysis of the Physical Punishment Component of a Parent Training Program. *Journal of Abnormal Child Psychology, 11,* 141–152.

This study is based on previous research that reveals that in order to change a child's behavior, "time-out" (lasting at least two minutes) is necessary. Compliments for good behavior or warnings do not result in positive behavior in a child.

The objective of this study is to examine what makes a child react positively to "time-out."

The study population consisted of two- to five-year-old children with behavioral problems.

When the children did not respond to "time-out," their parents were instructed to respond in one of two ways: spank the child on his behind or confine him to his room.

Both means helped, but the researchers do not recommend confinement, for fear of leaving an angry three-year-old child alone and unattended in his room.

Study 3:

Roberts, M.W. (1984). An Attempt to Reduce Time Out Resistance in Young Children. *Behavior Therapy*, *15*, 210–216.

Study population: kindergarteners with behavioral problems.

In the study, the researchers sought to examine if a parent can make do with a warning to force a child into a two-minute "time-out." This test is important to the researchers because previous studies show that this is the minimum punishment required for generating changes in behavior.

The parents tried to explain to the children what this was all about and to persuade them to cooperate. They even warned them and also demonstrated the sanctions the children would have to face if they didn't cooperate. The warnings and demonstrations had no effect on any of the children.

In other words, each child needed to experience punishment in a concrete manner at least once before cooperating with the command the next time. With most of the children, it took seven or eight times, and in the most extreme instance, it took sixteen times.

There was also a control group in this study in which the parents were supposed to ignore problematic behavior. This response did not lead to any improvement in the child's behavior.

In summary, the researcher wrote, "It would appear that children from this population need to experience punishment at least once in order to obey orders, despite the efforts of the therapists and parents to make do with warnings" (p. 216).

Study 4:

Roberts, M.W.,& Powers, S.W. (1990). Adjusting Chair Timeout Enforcement Procedures for Oppositional Children.*Behavior Therapy, 21*, 257–271.

This study deals with children of kindergarten age who had disciplinary problems and high levels of aggression. The researchers looked for the sanction that would force the children to comply with the parents' demand for "time-out."

The parents were divided into four groups:

Group 1: Parental response to the child getting up from the chair was a smack on the behind.

Group 2: Parental response was separating the child from the parent for a number of minutes, by way of placing a screen between them.

Group 3: The parent held the child in a way that prevented him from getting up from the chair.

Group 4: No sanction was given for getting up from the chair.

It appears from the study that only a smack on the behind, or the act of separating the child by way of a screen, made him cooperate with the "time-out" and subsequently improved his behavior. Holding the child (group 3) was of no use whatsoever. The behavior of the children who did not remain seated in the chair did not improve.

It should be noted that when parents were given a choice between the various sanctions, most of them preferred the smack on the behind.

Chapter 8, note number 1:

Freud, S. (1923). The Ego and the Id. *SE,*Vol. 19.

Freud, S. (1933). New Introductory Lectures on Psycho-analysis. *SE, 22*, 61–64, 163–164.

Freud locates the origins of the oedipal complex in the child's world of passions and fears. The strong will the child has to take his mother away from his father, and the subsequent fear of castration, are taken from the child's fantasy world. The oedipal complex is solved by identifying with the father, the strong oedipal enemy, and with his value system. This solution contributes to the establishment of the "superego." However, according to Freud, there is also a realistic side to these processes. The development of an ambivalent attitude toward the father springs from the child's mixed feelings toward his father; on the one hand, the father is a threatening oedipal enemy, and on the other hand, in the child's everyday life, he is also a concerned, caring, and loving father. The child's ambivalent attitude toward his father and the development of the superego are also the result of the child's parents' sets of demands and punishments that arouse his anger. In addition, the parents' practical demands and the threats of punishment, which in time are replaced by the threat of the loss of their love, are internalized as moral demands (when the threat of loss of love becomes a threat of guilty conscience) and thus also contribute to the development of the superego.

Chapter 8, note number 2:

Klein, M. (1946). Notes on Some Schizoid Mechanisms (pp. 1–24). In:*Envy and Gratitude and Other Works, 1946–1963*.London: Virago Press, 1988.

Klein, M. (1952). Some Theoretical Conclusions Regarding the Emotional Life of the Infant (pp. 61–93). In: *Envy and Gratitude and Other Works, 1946–1963*. London: Virago Press.

Klein, M. (1959). Our Adult World and Its Roots in Infancy. In: *Our Adult World*. New York: Basic Books, Inc., 1963.

Klein, M. (1937). Love, Guilt and Reparation (pp. 306–343). In:*Love, Guilt and Reparation and Other Works, 1921–1945*. New York: Dell Publishing Co., Inc., 1977.

Segal, H. (1989). *Klein*. The Institute of Psycho-Analysis. London: Karnac Books.

Chapter 8, note number 3:

According to Kleinian theory, the ability of a child to feel guilt, be aware of his aggression, and control it, depends on the extent to which he feels that he has been forgiven and the extent to which the mother is able to reduce the frustration that arouses his aggression.

In accordance with this theory, a baby, during the first two or three months of his life, does not relate to his mother as a complete human being, but rather as two separate entities—one bad (unsatisfactory), and the other good (satisfactory). A baby relates to the breast that provides him with his nourishment as an object and experiences the breast as split into two: the "good breast" (when the breast satisfies his hunger) and the "bad breast" (when he is hungry and not satisfied). The frustration vis-à-vis the "bad breast" arouses his **aggression,** which frightens him and is subsequently thrown outwardly at the world. Its repercussions hound him and he experiences the breast and the world as attacking him. This position of the baby is called the "paranoid-schizoid position," in which both adults and babies can find themselves. From this position, there is no possibility of recognizing aggression or taking responsibility for one's aggression, since it is perceived as originating in another person. As a result, the baby, the child, or the adult will not be able to regulate his behavior, he will experience the frustrating object as evil, and he will not hesitate to attack the object of his frustration.

According to Klein, the conceptual and cognitive maturity that takes place after the age of three months enables the baby to understand that the "bad" breast and the "good" breast are one. This is threatening, since the baby is afraid that his fantasized aggression toward the bad and frustrating object will destroy the good object (the hypothesis is that the baby, who lives in fantasy world, senses that his fantasy has a destructive power).

If the mother succeeds in ameliorating the baby's frustration at this stage, he will experience a decrease in aggression, be able to recognize it, and experience guilt and sorrow for feeling aggressive and desiring to hurt the object of his frustration. When parenting is benevolent, the baby will experience his aggression as bearable and repairable, since his mother has survived it. (The ability to repair means being able to appease and repair the harm caused to the object. According to Klein, during infancy a baby's ability to repair exists on a fantasy level and depends on the mother appearing once again as a benevolent object, after the moments of frustration and anger during which the baby imagines that he has destroyed her). Then the baby can experience himself as both good and bad and won't need to deny his aggression and discard it. In this way, a benevolent magic circle is formed. This magic circle generates the feeling that the other person is a whole, with good pieces and bad pieces. Alongside this, inhibitions develop and prevent harm from coming to frustrating objects. In other words, in accordance with this convoluted theory, a parent's forgiveness and the gratification it gives the child by softening his frustration facilitate the generation of inhibitions. On the other hand, parental criticism and toughness will be internalized by the child and he will experience these things as persecutory—it will become a part of him, a part that hounds him from within. In this case, he will feel that his anger and aggression are unbearable. He will fear his own anger, the world, and his peers. His experience of the world as a hostile place will increase his aggression, and the experience of the other as a threatening object will prevent him from conceiving the object as a whole, and will thus increase the processes of splitting, which will damage his ability to be considerate of the other. When the other frustrates him, he will not remember—on an emotional level—that the other is also good, and, in the absence of feelings of love and tenderness to balance and restrain the anger toward the other, he will attack him. In essence, according to Klein's theory, forgiveness, understanding, and acceptance are the building blocks of inhibitions.

Chapter 8, note number 4:

Klein, M. (1937). Love, guilt and reparation (pp. 318–319). In:*Love, Guilt and Reparation and Other Works*, 1921–1945. New York: Dell Publishing Co., 1977.

Immediately after that, Klein adds that problematic development could be an expression of a lack of parental love and thus expresses the ambivalence that apparently characterized her position toward the setting of boundaries for a child and frustrating him.

It is interesting to see that the aforementioned quote deals entirely with mothering as if Klein does not consider that fathering can also be significant to a child's development.

Chapter 8, note number 5:

Jacobson, E.M.D. (1965). *The Self and the Object World.* London: Hogarth Press and the Institute of Psycho-Analysis.

Jacobson agrees with Klein that the parents' total devotion to a baby during his first year of life, and their efforts to reduce his frustration to a minimum, enable him to develop feelings of guilt and real love. Without these, he will not be able to develop moral inhibitions. Nonetheless, Jacobson is convinced that this is just the first stage in the development of morality, whereas in the second stage, parental demands, criticism, anger, and punishment are of major importance. Through them, a child finds out when he should feel guilty, and how to restrain himself in order to avoid feelings of guilt (by way of boundaries). According to Jacobson, both stages are crucial in creating internal boundaries and a moral compass.

In other words, gentleness and love are **not enough** for a child to develop morality. Parents must also demand, criticize, and set boundaries. Moreover, not only will the internalized moral demands constitute a source of conflicts and feelings of guilt, but also a constant source of a sense of self-worth.

We agree with Jacobson on this. We think that the assumption of the Kleinians, that love for the significant other and the need of him (the result of gentle and devoted parenting) are sufficient to balance levels of the anger, disappointment, and constant search for thrills, is inaccurate. We believe that when a close and loving parent-child relationship also contains elements of boundary setting/enforcing, they are able to balance the intense anger and aggression that are evoked when the child is frustrated.

The Kleinian assumption is that the splitting processes, i.e., an adult's difficulty in maintaining a relationship with someone who frustrates him, spring from too much or too early frustration in the relationship with a parent, which leads to an inability to cope with a frustration-fraught relationship. We claim that a parent who is "too good" will not allow his child to experience ties with a realistic object, an object that is both satisfying and frustrating.

Chapter 8, note number 6:

Ogden, T.H. (1986). *The Matrix of the Mind*(pp. 131–165). Northvale, NJ, and London: Jason Aronson, Inc.

Chapter 8, note number 7:

Kohut, H. (1977). *The Restoration of the Self.* New York: International Universities Press, Inc.

Kohut, H. (1984). *How Does Analysis Cure?* Chicago and London: University of Chicago Press.

Kohut, H., & Seitz, P.F.D. (1963). Psychoanalytic Theory of Personality (pp. 113–141). In J.M. Wepman & R.W. Heine (Eds.), *Concepts of Personality.* Chicago: Aldine Publishing Company.

Kohut, H., & Wolf, E.S. (1978). The disorders of the self and their treatment: An outline. *International Journal of Psychoanalysis, 58*, 413–425.

Wolf, E.S. (1988). *Treating the Self.* New York and London: Guilford Press.

Kohut describes the self as consisting of two vertices: the grandiose self, which sprouts from the parents' ongoing wonder and empathy, and the ideal self, which consolidates in the process of joining with the parents' strength and serenity. Later on, the ideal self serves as a motivating power in self-fulfillment.

According to Kohut, the "superego" is not a restricting agent; rather, it pushes forward. Kohut claims that the destructive, violent, and furious aggression of a child or an adult is testimony to his frustration, due to the lack of understanding and empathy on the part of his parents. From this theoretical point of view, the solution to aggression lies in understanding the failure in empathy that generated aggression, and not by restricting it.

Kohut relates to boundaries with outspoken reservation. In his book *The Restoration of the Self* (p. 78), Kohut mentions the possibility that too much maternal "pampering" and empathy could be harmful to the child, since complete satisfaction does not allow development of a mature ego, sufficient control of the impulses, or sublimation, but he immediately backtracks and claims that such problems are infrequent.

For example, Kohut presents the case of a patient who was considered to have problems caused by overindulgence, but it transpired in the end that his problems were due to lack of empathy and lack of approval of his grandiose parts. On page 120 (ibid.) he writes that the parents' "no" is important in a child's development, because it provokes his anger and helps him to build his assertiveness—but still, Kohut disregards the importance of the "no" in building a child's moral inhibitions. Still, Kohut points out(ibid., p. 123) that a **pinch** of frustration does play an important role in teaching a child how to delay gratification.

In the epilog (p. 274) he claims that some parents never say "no" to their child due to their inability to bear the child's anger.

In all these writings, there is no mention of punishment, as if it is obvious to Kohut that it is not at all necessary.

In an earlier paper (1963) Kohut and Seitz warn that when the "no" is said firmly, it could cause a rigid repression in a child, which in the future will stop him from connecting with his repressed childish parts. Here, too, there is no mentioning of punishment.

In his book *How Does Analysis Cure?*, Kohut warns that a forbidding/rejecting response to a child's assertiveness will cause him to turn the assertiveness into destructiveness.

The essence of the Kohutian theory, which is characterized by emphasis on the importance of admiration and empathy, devaluation of limit setting, and strong rejection of criticism, made a substantial contribution to the resistance to boundary setting, which was typical of his time.

On the other hand, Wolf, one of Kohut's associates, thinks that the parents' job is to set boundaries and to be confrontational. He defines this parental function as "the adversarial function."

Wolf, E.S. (1988). *Treating the Self* (pp. 47, 55, 66–67). New York and London: Guilford Press.

It should be noted that with all his aversion to boundary setting, Kohut recognized how important it is to a child to experience parental power. According to him, a child's experience of merging with his parent's strength provides him with serenity and reduces the anxiety that he experienced as a small child facing the big world. In a paper he wrote with Wolf(1978), Kohut gives two examples of how a child may experience his parents' strength: when the parents hold him in their protecting arms as a baby, and when he hears his father telling the stories of his successful experiences in the army or at work. In his book *How Does Analysis Cure?*, he gives an example of how the cuddling of a child by his mother enables him to merge with her strength and serenity. Another way of transferring to a child a sense of strength and calm is to react calmly to environmental stimuli.

However, unlike Jacobson, Masterson, and Erikson, Kohut does not make the connection between boundary setting and a child's experience of his parents' strength. The question that arises is this: Is a child who defies his parents and pays no attention to what they say able to experience them as being strong? Are a hug, success stories, and serenity sufficient to pass on a message of parental strength?

Chapter 9, note number 1:

Lyons, J.S. & Larzelere, R.E. (1996). Where is evidence that non-abusive corporal punishment increases aggression? Paper presented at the XXVI International Congress of Psychology, Montreal.

In 1979, the Swedish parliament, in an effort to prevent child abuse, passed a law forbidding corporal punishment.

Did it actually stop child abuse or should the dramatic rise in violence in Sweden be blamed on this law?

It is hard to examine this question directly, since there is insufficient data on this subject in Sweden prior to 1979. Attempts are therefore being made to examine this subject indirectly. In 1981 a study compared the levels of violence in the United States and violence in Sweden during the 1960s and 1970s. Students were asked if, during their childhood and youth, they had been spanked by their parents in a way that left a mark on their bodies that lasted longer than ten minutes. Nine and a half percent of American students who participated in the survey answered in the affirmative, compared with two percent of Swedish students. The researchers concluded that during the 1960s and 1970s, the level of child abuse was lower in Sweden than in the United States.

In contrast, when a comparison was made between the situation in the United States (a survey from 1985) and that in Sweden after legislation against corporal punishment (1980), it transpired that in comparison with American parents, Swedes gave fewer disciplinary spankings but administered significantly more brute force and violence.

In light of these statistics, the researchers concluded that ultimately, a complete ban on disciplinary spanking increases the likelihood of harsher parental violence. Their hypothesis was that when a parent refrains from responding to his child's annoying behavior with a disciplinary spank at the appropriate moment, the result is that the child continues with this behavior and the parent's increasing anger will ultimately cause him to respond in a much more brutal manner.

Moreover, the researchers presented statistical data from the Swedish police that deal with abused children under the age of seven. The statistics indicate a 627 percent increase in attacks by juveniles against other juveniles from 1981 (two years after enactment of the law) to 1994. The researchers make a connection between this law and that horrendous rise, and are convinced that damaged parental authority is responsible for the increased violence.

Chapter 9, note 2:

According to 4596/98: Anonymous vs. the State of Israel.

Chapter 10, note number 1:

The five studies displayed here are relatively recent. Two of them are accompanied by criticisms sent to journals by research doctors.

Straus, M.A. (2000). Corporal punishment of children and adult depression and suicidal ideation. In M.A. Straus & D.A. Donnelly, *Beating the Devil Out of Them: Corporal Punishment in American Families and Its Effects on Children.* New Brunswick, NJ: Transaction Publications.

Straus, M.A., & Yodanis, C.L. (1996). Corporal punishment in adolescence and physical assaults on spouses later in life: What accounts for the link? *Journal of Marriage and the Family*, 58, 825–841.

Ullman, A., & Straus, M.A. (In Press). Violence by Children against mothers in relation to violence between parents and corporal punishment by parents. *Journal of Comparative Family Studies, 34*, 41–60.

MacMillan, H.L., Boyle, M.H., Wong, M.Y., Duku, E.K., Fleming, J.E., & Walsh, C.A. (1999). Slapping and spanking in childhood and its association with lifetime prevalence of psychiatric disorders in a general population sample. *Canadian Medical Association Journal, 17*(17), 805–809.

MacMillan's study examines the connection between corporal punishment and the development of anxiety, depression, addiction, alcohol abuse, and issues of aggression. The study demonstrates that there is a connection between issues of aggression and addiction and corporal punishment in childhood/adolescence. Nonetheless, since the participants in the study were adults who were asked about events that took place during their childhood and teenage years, the researchers themselves agree that there is a problem with the results. It is quite possible that the population that did not suffer from depression, addiction, or aggression had also been subjected to physical punishment before the age of three to four years (the time during which 90 percent of parents spanked their children), except that most people don't remember events that took place before the age of five, which is why this was not expressed in the study.

Straus, M.A., Sugarman, D.B., & Giles-Sims, J. (1997). Spanking by Parents and Subsequent antisocial behavior of children. *Archives of Pediatrics and Adolescent Medicine, 151*, 761–767.

This study examines the connection between physical punishment, administered to a child by his mother, and the level of his aggression. Mothers were asked if they smacked their children during the past week and how many times. Children were divided into three age groups of three to five years, six to nine years, and ten years. The study reveals that there is a connection between the spankings the children received and their level of aggression two years later.

Smith, D.H. (2000). A letter to the editor. *Canadian Medical Association Journal, 162,* 757.

Criticism of MacMillan et al.'s commentary on the results of their study:

There is an additional hypothesis to explain the connection between parental spanking and psychiatric problems. It is possible that aggressive behavior at a young age is connected to a trait that increases the feasibility of psychiatric problems at a later stage.

Another point that is ignored by the researchers is the fact that there is no comparison between the danger to a child from a smack on the behind and the danger to a child who is out of control. "In my work," says Smith, "I, myself, get to be present in situations, where parents need to apply physical punishment in order to control their disruptive children." Under these circumstances he advises parents to restrict themselves to a smack on the behind, and **not** to do this at the peak of their anger.

Whatley, P. (2000). A letter to the editor. *Canadian Medical Association Journal, 162,* 757.

Whatley also criticizes MacMillan et al.'s interpretation of their results. He claims that the causal connection they note between disciplinary spanking during childhood and the development of psychiatric problems is based on the interpretation of memories that adults have of their early childhood (which is not necessarily an objective analysis).

Isaacs, R.L. (2000). A letter to the editor. *Canadian Medical Association Journal*, *162*, 758.

Isaacs criticizes the research of MacMillan et al. He points out that the researchers themselves admit that they did not take into account many mediating variables in the study population: alcoholic parents, parents with psychiatric problems, poverty, size of family, socioeconomic status, and educational concepts.

Prins, L. (2000). A Letter to the Editor. *Canadian Association Journal*, *162*, 758.

Prins, too, criticizes MacMillan et al.'s research because they claim that statistics point to a causality in a certain direction. Prins claims that there is possibly a mediating variable that could explain the statistics. It might be, he says, that children with inner turmoil and high energetic level arouse more anger in their parents and have a greater chance of being punished. Similarly, children with these character traits have a greater chance of developing psychiatric problems in adulthood

Ambati, B.K., Ambati, J., & Rao, A.M. (1998). A letter to the editor. *Archives of Pediatrics and Adolescent Medicine*, *152*, 303.

These doctors criticize the research conducted by Straus, Sugarman, and Giles-Sims. They claim that the study does not take into consideration the effect of significant mediating variables, such as absence of a father, a single-parent family, and the person delivering the smack (father as opposed to mother). Furthermore, they warn of severe problems in the statistical analysis on which the researchers relied when analyzing the data and the results. According to Ambati et al., even if these problems are ignored, the statistical correlation between physical punishment and antisocial behavior (in this study) is only 10 percent.

According to Ambati et al., reality itself contradicts the researchers' claims. There has been a significant drop in the legitimacy of physical punishment since 1950 and at the same time there has been a dramatic rise in juvenile crime.

Larzelere, R.E., Baumrind, D., &Polite, K. (1998). Emerging perspectives of parental spanking from two 1996 conferences. *Archives of Pediatrics and Adolescent Medicine, 152*, 303–305.

The researchers refer to two conferences that took place in 1996 and examine the issue of disciplinary spanking in the United States.

They point to the studies presented at these conferences, which differentiated between disciplinary spanking and actual abuse, a differentiation that is missing in earlier studies.

Eight of the studies presented at the conferences found that a disciplinary spanking led to a reduction in violent behavior among children, especially if the spank on the behind was used to back up softer approaches to punishment and if the child was older than two years and younger than six years.

It transpired during these conferences that today there are two main approaches to the issue of punishment in regard to disciplinary spanking. One approach completely opposes any use of physical punishment, whereas the other approach claims that a disciplinary spanking is an appropriate means of punishment and is effective in certain circumstances.

The three researchers are especially critical toward the aforementioned study by Straus, Sugarman, and Giles-Sims (ibid.), which looks at the effect of disciplinary spanking on children aged between six and nine years.

In this study, parents were split into two groups, "spankers" and "non-spankers." The criteria were as follows: A mother had to answer the question "Have you spanked your child during the last week?" A negative response placed her in the "non-spanking" group and her child was placed in the group of the "non-spanked." Larzelere, Baumrind, and Polite claim that because of the design of the study, the children who were spanked less than once a week entered the group of the "non-spanked," which also included children who had been spanked before the age of six and were already aware of their parents' authority and respected their demands. Therefore, the researchers claim, their parents no longer needed to resort to physical punishment.

Furthermore, Larzelere et al. claim that the statistical data from the study itself indicate that the only group that demonstrated that disciplinary spanking raised the levels of aggression was the group of the six- to nine-year-olds who were spanked at least three times a week and occasionally even daily.

Chapter 10, note number 2:

Baumrind, D. (1996). A blanket injunction against disciplinary use of spanking is not warranted by the data. *Pediatrics*, *99*(4), 828–831.

This publication is part of a debate on disciplinary spanking. Diana Baumrind, a veteran researcher in the field of education, condemns a blanket injunction against the use of spanking as a parental disciplinary means. She bases her claims on the results of various studies (references can be found in the paper itself). According to Baumrind, the efficacy of methods for imposing discipline, including a disciplinary spanking, rely on the level of **legitimacy** provided by the environment.

Just explaining is not sufficient in enforcing boundaries, claims Baumrind, and on occasion it is necessary to punish, since children learn how to behave from their parents' response, including administration of punishment when necessary.

In cases of defiant children, an aversive response increases the efficacy of a relatively light punishment, such as "time-out." A brief explanation, before or after punishment, helps a child to understand the context of the punishment and to control the behavior that brought about the punishment.

Punishment (including physical punishment) does not weaken the internalization of adult values; on the contrary, it reinforces them, says Baumrind.

A direct instruction and concrete punishment (physical included) help a child learn to control his behavior. When parents refrain from such direct means and resort to emotional manipulation, rejection, and alienation, a child experiences anxiety and guilt and his critical thinking is harmed.

Since it is natural for parental control to diminish rather than increase during a child's adolescence, it is necessary to establish clear and stable habits of good behavior during infancy. To this end, it is usually necessary to administer stricter discipline.

As for the claim that disciplinary spanking at this age will make a child violent, says Baumrind, children understand that their rights and obligations are not the same as their parents', and just as children understand that they are not required to go to work like their parents, so do they understand that getting spanked by their parents does not give them permission to attack their peers. Baumrind adds that when a disciplinary spank is administered within the framework of a stable family, it helps discipline a child, whereas a disciplinary spank administered within a framework of an unstable family is of no use. This claim is based on studies conducted in an African American community, studies in a community of laborers (which gives legitimacy to this kind of punishment), and studies conducted in a white community.

Baumrind claims that parents who oppose the use of fierce punitive measures, such as disciplinary spanking, raise children who are more aggressive, whereas families who make some use of disciplinary spanking (not every day) raise children who are less aggressive than the others.

Moreover, according to Baumrind, if a child's aggression is not restrained, his violence will increase. She presents cases of hyperactive children, for whom it has been found that punishment reduces hyperactivity, whereas positive reinforcement brings about no change at all.

Baumrind says that parents who use punishment, not as a means for releasing anger, but as a disciplinary measure, appear to cause no harm, whereas parents who object to physical punishment sometimes tend to explode and beat their children uncontrollably, and cause significant harm. Baumrind makes a connection between this particular response and the "pattern of responsive outburst" to which Patterson refers to as having harmful consequences.

Baumrind claims that it is not the disciplinary spanking that leads to aggression among children, but the other way around—rude and aggressive children arouse their parents' anger; as a result, they respond by spanking them.

Grusec, J.E., & Goodnow, J.J. (1994). Impact of parental discipline methods on the child's internalization of values: A Reconceptualization of Current points of view.*Developmental Psychology*, *30*, 4–19.

This paper touches on the question of whether punishment, such as disciplinary spanking, eases the internalization of moral values. The authors claim that this depends on whether the disciplinary means are conceived by the child as being legitimate; in other words, whether the punishment has the approval of the child's environment. Since most of the studies in this field are conducted on white middle-class populations, say the authors, these disciplinary means are not useful because they get little legitimacy from the environment.

The authors hypothesize that legitimacy of punishment depends on the gender of the person who punishes. They quote from a study that claims that among children aged between three and eight years, punishment imposed by the father gets more legitimacy.

Larzelere, R.E. (1996). A Review of the Outcomes of Parental Use of Nonabusive or Customary Physical Punishment. *Pediatrics*, *98*(4), 842–828.

Larzelere draws attention to the problems that arise when interpretation of the studies conclude that spanking is harmful. According to him, a large proportion of these studies do not differentiate between abuse and disciplinary spanking, and it so happens that studies that look at the effects of abuse on a child are presented as studies that confirm that disciplinary spanking is harmful.

Moreover, according to Larzelere, in most of the studies (twenty-seven out of thirty-five) in the aforementioned review, no attention was paid to a child's aggression levels or his behavioral disturbances before he was punished, which makes it impossible to examine whether or not these were exacerbated by the punishment.

Eight studies, conducted on children aged between two and six, examine the level of behavioral disturbances in a child before and after his parents' response. It was found that physical punishment lowers the level of the disturbance. Among older children, confinement was found to be effective in disciplining the child, while nine other forms of sanctions exacerbated the behavior.

Contrary to the effect on children, physical punishment, administered to youths, was found to be harmful.

Polite, K. (1996). The medium/the message: Corporal punishment, an empirical critique. *Pediatrics, 98*(4), 849–851.

The researchers A.M. Graziano, J.L. Hamblen, and W.A. Plante claim that the results of their study—"Subabusive violence in child rearing in middle-class American families," published in *Pediatrics*, volume 98(4), pages 845–848—confirm that all forms of physical punishment must be banned, since such punishment arouses children's anger, resentment, and sadness.

Polite, on the other hand, claims that if punishment fails to arouse feelings of sorrow or anger in a child, the punishment does not fulfill its duty.

In the aforementioned study by Polite, it was found that 93 percent of all parents questioned said that they use physical punishment occasionally. They claimed that this punishment was effective. Nonetheless, they reported that they experienced conflicting feelings with regard to their use of punishment.

According to Polite, the reason that so many parents resort to occasional physical punishment, despite their conflicting emotions, is the ineffectiveness of other disciplinary means.

Gunnoe, M.I., & Mariner, C.L. (1997). Toward a Developmental-Contextual Model of the Effects of Parental Spanking on Children's Aggression. *Archives of Pediatrics and Adolescent Medicine, 151*(8), 768–775.

At the beginning of the article, the authors relate to the American Academy of Pediatrics and the Maternal and Child Health Bureau conference that was held in 1996 and dealt with disciplinary measures. Here, in brief, are the conclusions:

There is a consensus among various researchers that disciplinary spanking is not suitable for a child younger than two years or older than eleven years.

As for the effect of this punishment on children aged between two and eleven years, opinions differ. Some people claim that it encourages the use of violence to solve problems, and others claim that the effect of a disciplinary spank depends on the circumstances under which it is administered and its significance for the child.

Gunnoe and Mariner conducted a study that deals with the effect of disciplinary spanking on children's aggression. The study compared children of various ages and also compared African American families with white families. The children were aged between seven and eleven years, and the study followed them for over five years. The children's preliminary level of aggression was taken into consideration, and then the extent of the children's involvement in schoolyard fights, and levels of their antisocial behavior were measured.

The results show that there is a correlation between physical punishment and a rise in aggression in only one group: boys aged over eight years who have single mothers. The researchers hypothesize that this is due to the mother's inability to maintain authority since children tend to perceive males as more authoritarian.

Disciplinary spanking, administered to boys under the age of six in African American families, reduced aggression. The researchers credit this to the fact that African American families give more legitimacy to physical punishment, so that it is easier for parents to continue to exhibit warmth toward a child after punishing him, since the parents are not shocked by what they did.

Gunnoe and Mariner claim that when a child sees disciplinary spanking as a legitimate expression of parental authority, this will reduce his aggression, and vice versa. Legitimacy depends on family norms, family hierarchy, and the extent to which a child perceives the punishing parent as a person of authority. For this reason, a child's age is significant and there is a consensus that at the age of seven years, a child's concept of adult authority undergoes a change.

Chapter 10, note number 3:

Larzelere, R.E. (2000) Child outcomes of nonabusive and customary physical punishment by parents: An updated literature review. *Clinical Child and Family Psychology Review*, 3(4), 199–221.

This paper reviews almost forty studies conducted on the effects of disciplinary spanking of children.

The conclusions state that there are situations in which a disciplinary spanking is harmful just as there are situations in which it is not harmful and even beneficial to a child's education. Larzelere indicates the conditions under which it mostly isn't harmful and is even beneficial: 1) Spanking is on the behind. 2) The child is older than two years or younger than six years. 3) Spanking is administered by warm, concerned, and loving parents. 4) Spanking is not given out of a loss of control. 5) This kind of punishment is used infrequently. 6) Spanking is not too hard.

The paper contains statistical data from a review conducted in Sweden fifteen years after a law against corporal punishment was enacted. It appears from the data that the legislation resulted in a drastic reduction in previous support for disciplinary spanking and this did indeed lead to reduced use of this disciplinary measure. On the other hand, however, the pattern of hair pulling, shoving, kicking, and beating did not lessen in the wake of the law.

Larzelere claims that the law did indeed deter parents from giving their children disciplinary spankings (e.g., a spank on the behind) at an early age, but this resulted in uninhibited youngsters who had no respect for parental authority. This situation calls for parents, exhausted from concern and anger, to quickly lose their temper and lash out uncontrollably.

Chapter 10, note number 4:

Larzelere, R.E., Schneider, W.N., Larson, D.B., & Pike, P.L. (1996). The Effects of Discipline Responses in Delaying Toddler Misbehavior Recurrences. *Child and Family Behavior Therapy*, *18*, 35–37.

Chapter 10, note number 5:

DiLalla, L.F., Mitchell, C.M., Arthur, M.W., & Pagliocca, P.M. (1988). Aggression and delinquency: Family and environmental factors. *Journal of Youth and Adolescence*, *17*(3), 233–246.

Study population: Teenagers caught carrying out criminal activity with various levels of aggression.

The study examines the effect of parental disciplinary measures, as well as the effect of peers on levels of aggression and criminal tendencies.

The researchers hypothesized that the more fierce and more aggressive the measures of punishment used by parents, the higher the level of aggression among their teenage children (as expressed in the home, in school, and through the children's criminal activity).

Three levels of parental discipline were determined.

1) Parents had not punished the boy at all throughout his childhood and adolescent years; they only spoke to him and explained to him how he should behave.

2) Parents administered discipline by confinement or denying privileges.

3) Parents responded to unruly behavior by shouting at the child or spanking his behind.

The results of the study surprised the researchers. It appears that the most violent boys in school were those who were treated most gently by their parents.

In other words, **the gentler the parental approach, the higher the level of violence.** The other two levels of parental discipline did not differ from each other in their effect.

Chapter 10, note number 6:

Gordon, E. (2001). Judges Without Boundaries. *Tchelet: A Journal of Israeli Thought.*

Evelyn Gordon quotes legal and research studies against the ruling of Justice Beinish. According to her, important studies published in recent years indicate that physical punishment that does not constitute any kind of abuse is an especially effective method for forcing discipline. Gordon goes on to say that the abovementioned ruling is based on weak legal reasoning. Incrimination of common behavior, she claims, might be disastrous, both to family law and to the rule of law. Gordon also stresses that seventy-six out of eighty-four of the democratic states in the world choose not to interfere in parents' right to use moderate physical punishment for the purpose of educating their children.

Chapter 11, note number 1:

Weinblatt, A. (1999). Rehabilitating Parental Authority. An M.A. Thesis in Social Sciences, Tel Aviv University. The Department of Social Sciences.

Weinblatt deals with the gloomy consequences of the loss of parental authority. He refers to the term "reverse hierarchy," which describes a situation in which a child, who in reality depends on his parents for his existence and welfare, accumulates power and starts to control them inappropriately. In such a situation, the entire family system is in denial of the natural hierarchy that should exist within a family structure.

Chapter 12, note number 1

Benjamin, J. (1995). Recognition and destruction: An outline of intersubjectivity. In *Like Subjects, Love Objects: Essays on Recognition and Sexual Difference*. New Haven: Yale University Press.

Benjamin reminds us that around one year of age, at the first stage of rapprochement, an infant begins to understand that he and his mother are separate and that his mother has a will of her own. At this point in time, the mother also begins to sense that the baby's demands are not only an expression of his needs, but also an expression of his independent (tyrannical) will. In this respect, Benjamin relates to the issue of power struggle between mother and child, when together and also when separated.

Chapter 12, note number 2:

Jacobson, E.M.D. (1965). *The Self and the Object World.* London: Hogarth Press and the Institute of Psycho-Analysis.

Masterson, J.F. (1985). *Treatment of the Borderline Adolescent: A Developmental Approach.* New York: Brunner/Mazel Publishers.

Price, J.F. (1996). *Power and Compassion.* New York and London: Guilford Press.

Both Jacobson and Masterson are convinced that a child needs to feel that his parent is strong and that he gets this feeling if the parent is present and ready to set boundaries and confront him.

Jacobson claims that at a certain stage in a child's development, the main issues cease to be "bad" vs. "good" and become "strong" vs. "weak". This developmental leap has implications for a child's attitude toward his parents and explains why he can stand frustration, an affront to his sense of freedom, and even aggression from his parents, rather than bear their weakness. A child's recognition of his weakness, and the understanding that he depends on his parents, reinforces his yearning for them to be strong.

Jerome Price, the psychotherapist and instructor who established the Michigan Family Institute and member of the Family Therapy Institute in Washington, D.C., also stresses that a child feels more secure if he experiences his parent as a strong figure, and this can happen only if the parents run the house, not the child.

Chapter 14, note number 1:

Kahn, M.M.R. (1969). On Symbiotic Omnipotence. *Psychoanalytic Forum, 3*, 137–147.

Chapter 16, note number 1:

Benjamin, J. (1988). *The Bonds of Love* (pp. 33–35, 38–39). New York: Pantheon Books.

Jessica Benjamin, a contemporary psychoanalyst, reckons that parents find it hard to set boundaries for their children if they don't believe that their children are able to bear this experience. A parent will overindulge his child when he senses that his child is unable to bear frustration or disappointment, or when he himself is unable to bear the guilt of frustrating his child.

Overindulgence of children can be harmful, since it leaves children with a sense of absolute power and prevents them from recognizing their real power. Even worse, such children will not be considerate of their parents and won't experience them as separate from themselves. As a result, children will be unable to feel that someone else, separate from themselves, is able to love them and, notwithstanding all the gentleness and acceptance heaped on them by their parents, they will still feel lonely and desolate.

Overindulgence on the part of the parent generates relations that are devoid of real closeness. Children do not learn to be considerate of other people and do not regard them as separate individuals, but rather as objects that are there to serve them.

Chapter 19, note number 1:

A similar view of this mental dynamic can be seen in Professor Haim Omer's book, *Non-Violent Resistance*, published in Hebrew by Modan in 2002.

Chapter 19, note number 2:

An example of this approach:

Bruch, H. (1988). *Conversations with Anorexics*. New York: Basic Books, Inc.

Hilda Bruch, one of the first theoreticians on the subject of eating disorders, is convinced that anorexic girls' parents are too demanding and intrusive and, from early childhood, the girls feel the need to appease their parents at the cost of ignoring their own needs and aspirations. These girls are afraid to be spontaneous and natural and internalize their parents' extreme and harsh control over them. This is expressed in the way they relate to their own bodies, and the extreme self-discipline and strict control they impose on themselves.

Dr. Eitan Bachar—author of the book *The Fear of Grabbing a Place: Anorexia and Bulimia: Therapy in line with the "theory of the self,"* published by Magnus Press at the Hebrew University in Jerusalem—makes a connection between avoidance of food and empathy deprivation.

According to the theory of the self, optimal development needs a sufficiently empathetic environment and a strong parental figure.

Bachar claims that a girl who develops an eating disorder is deprived of such an environment. Throughout her childhood, this particular parental child is empathetic toward her weak parents, fulfills their needs, and alleviates their depressive feelings, disregarding her own needs in favor of her parents'. This explains why the anorexic girl feels guilty whenever she deals with her own needs and takes up space in the world. Since eating is conceived as an act of selfishness and pampering, the anorexic will fast and the bulimic will vomit.

According to this theory, the attitude that anorexics develop toward food is similar to their attitude toward the absent significant other. Food represents security, comfort, and warmth that should have been received from a significant other.

Another explanation for self-starvation relates to a girl's mother's failure to exhibit warmth and love during the child's critical developmental stages, at the basis of which lies the hypothesis that the mother in question is controlling and surrender is the price the child has to pay for having a relationship with her.

Sugarman, A.,Quinlan, D., & Devenis, L. (1981). Anorexia Nervosa as a defense against Anaclitic Depression. *International Journal of Eating Disorders, 1*, 44–61.

The authors' explanation for the development of anorexia is based on the separation- individuation theory. According to this theory, an anorexic's mother is unable to enjoy her child's developing abilities, when she is still in the practicing stage, and reacts to them with alienation. She does not provide a "safe basis" for the child, and as a result, the daughter develops a fear of losing her beloved mother. During adolescence, when the girl is once again facing separation from her mother, she becomes intensely anxious and, since her mother is represented by food, the girl tries to connect to her through eating, and immediately afterward to separate from her through vomiting. The significance of anorexia is a denial of the need for a mother. We could say that these children's difficulties are caused by their mothers' need to control and by the fact that any close relationship with them can be maintained only at the price of surrender to their demands.

Chapter 20, note number 1:

Widom, C.S. (1989). Does violence beget violence? A Critical Examination of the Literature. *Psychological Bulletin, 106*(1), 3–28.

In this paper, Widom reviews studies that deal with the issue of childhood abuse in relation to violence resulting later in life. The conclusion is that most abusive parents did not experience abuse during their childhoods. Some studies state that adults who experience abuse during childhood will be aggressive later in life, some have opposite results, and some state that there is no connection between the two variables.

There is a methodological problem in these studies since there is no definition for parental violence in the paper. It is therefore possible that parents who use a spank on the behind as a disciplinary means were placed in the same category as parents who use brutal disciplinary means.

Chapter 20, note number 2:

Rieffe, P. (1966). *The Triumph of the Therapeutic*. Chicago and London: University of Chicago Press.

Chapter 20, note number 3:

Taub, G. (1997). *A Dispirited Rebellion.* (pp. 215–109). Hakibbutz Hameuhad Publishers. (Hebrew)

Chapter 20, note number 4:

Patterson, G.R. (1982). *Coercive Family Process.* Eugene, OR: Castalia Press.

Patterson, G.R., & Stouthamer-Loeber, M. (1984). The Correlation of Family Management Practices and Delinquency. *Child Development, 55*, 1299–1307.

This study examines the connection between four different patterns of parental behavior and juvenile delinquency.

The patterns are:

The extent of parental supervision: What do they know about their child's activities, and how closely do they supervise him?

The type of discipline: Mainly punishments such as "time-out" and denial of privileges, with special attention given to parents' consistency.

The extent to which parents are helping their child with problem solving.

The extent to which the child is given positive reinforcements.

Study population: Children in seventh and eighth grade.

Children's delinquency was determined according to their own reports as well as police reports.

The study concludes that children's delinquency is influenced only by the extent of their parents' supervision and the kind of punishment that they were subjected to. No significant correlation was found between delinquency and the level of positive reinforcements that children received from their parents, or the help they received with problem solving.

Patterson, G.R., DeGarmo, D.S., & Knutson, N. (2000). Hyperactive and antisocial behaviors: Comorbid or two points in the same process? *Development and Psychopathology, 12*, 91–106.

This study deals with the effects of parental patterns of punishing on their child's transition from being hyperactive to becoming antisocial. Both hyperactive and antisocial children have two typical behavioral patterns: 1) Coercive type of behavior (lack of discipline, temper tantrums, and other unacceptable behaviors). 2) Deficiency in social skills.

The researchers assume that inappropriate parental disciplinary measures will be characteristic of both a hyperactive child and an antisocial child.

The independent factor was a child's temperament. According to the researchers, when a temperamental infant with "temper tantrums" meets a non-contingent parent, the chances are that with time the child will develop antisocial behavior.

The term "non-contingent parent" is used to describe a parent who on one hand does not punish his child for his unruly behavior, and on the other hand does not positively reinforce his child for pro-social behavior. (Patterson uses the term "negative reinforcement" in relation to punishment.)

The researchers attach great importance to boundaries and discipline, in light of data that show that lack of discipline, combined with social skills deficiency, places children at a high risk of failing in school and being rejected by peers (they are not easy on the environment and hard to control in the classroom). When effective disciplinary measures were used, a positive change in the child's behavior, and subsequently, a reduction of social rejection, were observed.

Another assumption in the study is that hyperactivity frequently precedes delinquent behavior.

And this is how it happens: When a hyperactive and temperamental infant encounters a non-contingent parent, chances are that the child will become high-strung, undisciplined, and uncooperative. At two years old, such a toddler will suffer from outbursts of anger and his behavior will be unpleasant. He will snatch things from his friends, won't listen to anyone, and may even develop a linguistic problem due to his use of physical force, rather than verbal cooperation (linguistic problems can be the cause rather than the effect).

The researchers' hypothesis is that an outburst of anger in a three-year-old, violence in an eight-year-old, and drug abuse and early imprisonment in adolescence are all the consequences of the encounter between a hyperactive and temperamental child and a parent with ineffective, uncoordinated, and erratic disciplinary patterns.

The researchers' assumptions were confirmed a corrclation between hyperactivity and antisocial behavior was found. Further, the researchers found that a change in parental disciplinary patterns brought about a significant and dramatic reduction in the transition from hyperactivity to antisocial behavior, which happened in a short time.

Another risk to the development of antisocial behavior in children is parents who themselves present with antisocial behavior. The researchers assume that the reason is that such parents do not punish their children for their deviant behavior, such as physical violence, theft, and threats, and sometimes even encourage it, mainly because they don't categorize such behavior as out of the ordinary. This assumption is based on the results of two earlier studies.

This study also finds that the second most important factor in youth antisocial behavior is peer group influence.

According to Reid, Snyder, and Patterson's current model, ineffective parental response is a major predicting factor of negative behavior in all age groups. In late childhood, another predicting factor is susceptibility to the influence of peers.

Chapter 20, note number 5:

Denham, S.A. et al. (2000). Prediction of externalizing behavior problems from early to middle childhood: The role of parental socialization and emotion expression. *Development and Psychopathology, 12*, 23–45.

This is a longitudinal study concerning the treatment of kindergarteners with behavioral disturbances, aggression, and problems with discipline. The authors quote thirteen studies from the 1990s. Results show that early aggression is the first stage in a process that leads to long-term antisocial behavior. According to the authors, among many children, behavioral disorders remain stable throughout the years, so that it is necessary to diagnose them at kindergarten age.

This specific study examines the effects of three different parental approaches on a child's behavior: 1) Setting boundaries. 2) Support in carrying out chores. 3) Showing positive emotions toward the child.

The researchers were surprised to find that demonstration of positive emotions had no positive effect on children. In contrast, however, support in carrying out chores through boundary setting succeeded in putting an end to behavioral disturbances. Children who were not treated in this manner remained behaviorally disturbed.

Chapter 20, note number 6:

Freud assumes that aggression is inherent and that social and cultural restrictions are made with the intention to prevent its imposition on others.

Freud, S. (1933). New Introductory Lectures on Psycho-analysis. Lecture 32: Anxiety and instinctual life. *SE, 22*, 81–111.

Freud, S. (1923). The Ego and the Id. *SE, 19*.

Klein and Kohut, too, understand that aggression is inherent (see previous notes), but they believe that its destructiveness can be influenced to a large extent by an empathetic parent.

Chapter 20, note number 7:

See reference to Thomas Ogden's theory in Chapter 8.

Chapter 21, note number 1:

Patterson, G.R. (1982). Maternal rejection: Determinant or product for deviant child behavior? In W. Hartup & Z. Rubin (Eds.), *Relationship and Development* (pp. 73–94). Hillsdale, NJ, and London: Laurence Erlbaum Associates.

This study by Patterson follows previous studies that note a correlation between failure in mother-child relations and adjustment problems in adulthood, antisocial behavior, alcoholism, crime, and problems in the workplace and in marriage.

Patterson wanted to examine the issue of the chicken and the egg—whether maternal rejection leads to aggression and social problems in children, or the opposite, that children's unpleasant behavior leads to being rejected by their mothers.

In contrast to what was accepted at the time, Patterson hypothesizes that it is a child's unpleasant behavior that arouses his mother's rejection, as follows: The mother attempts to set boundaries, but she encounters a stormy response from her son, which causes her to step back. The child then senses that this is the way to get what he wants. Thus, a parent's conciliatory attitude reinforces her child's aggressive behavior.

The harsher the conflicts around disciplining the child—because of his difficult temperament—the harder the mother tries to avoid them. When the mother shies away from conflicts and fails to discipline the child, he will exacerbate his antisocial behavior, which results in more conflicts and more temper tantrums, demands, beating, and vexation.

As a result of this vicious cycle, the mother will develop feelings of revulsion toward her child.

Thus Patterson concludes that maternal rejection is the result of a child's antisocial behavior at home, which confirms his first hypothesis.

The study also examines the question of whether a child's failure in school and the mother's disappointment are the reasons for rejecting him. This was not found to be significant.

On the other hand, Patterson found a correlation between lack of discipline at home and a child's problems in school. His hypothesis is that a child's "success" in maintaining his unruly behavior and control over his parents through aggressive behavior encourages him to continue this behavior in school, which leads to his rejection by his peers

Chapter 22, note number 1:

Dobson, J. (1970). *Dare to Discipline*. Wheaton, IL: Tyndale House Publishers.

Dr. James Dobson, a psychologist and former teacher, wrote a book that is a sort of a response to Dr. Spock's permissive approach. According to Dobson, childhood is a critical period for setting boundaries and establishing parental authority.

He explains that during adolescence, children are more susceptible to potentially dangerous temptations such as drugs, running away from home, and sex. It is therefore important that boundaries and parental authority have already been internalized by the time a child reaches this age. It is no good waiting until the child reaches adolescence in order to set boundaries for him, he says, since at this age there is a natural increase in rebelliousness and the child who has already learned to ignore his parents' demands cannot be expected to start listening to them during his teenage years.

Fearless Parenting Makes Confident Kids is based on the authors' vast experience in the field of behavioral and psychiatric disorders in children and adolescents.

Shulamit Blank, M.D., is a pediatrician and child and adolescent psychiatrist. She is the founder and, since 1993, CEO of Bnei Arazim, a community-based educational and residential treatment facility in Rishon LeZion for children and adolescents with severe psychiatric and behavioral disorders.

Dr. Blank successfully implements her methods at the facility, which is composed of a special school, daycare center, family therapy unit, and emergency unit. With support from her team of teachers, youth leaders, social workers, physical therapists, and family therapists, she rehabilitates children, prevents psychiatric hospitalization and incarceration, and minimizes the use of psychiatric drugs through education, sports, and setting appropriate boundaries tailored to each child's specific issues, such as A.D.H.D., learning disabilities, aggression, and anxiety.

She has three children and seven grandchildren and resides with her spouse near Tel Aviv.

Orly Fuchs-Shabtai is a clinical psychologist and since 2006 has been the director of a national program (*Ilanot*) for the prevention of child violence that operates in twenty-five cities in Israel. The program, run by thirty-five counselors from therapeutic fields, deals with training educational staff and parents in setting boundaries for children with behavioral disorders and provides counseling to hundreds of families and teachers each year.

The author is the mother of three and lives in Tel Aviv.

The authors strive to follow the ancient wisdom of the biblical aphorism: *"Train up a child in the way he should go and when he is old he will not depart from it"* (Proverbs 22:6).

Made in the USA
Charleston, SC
04 October 2016